☑ W9-CND-339

DISCARD

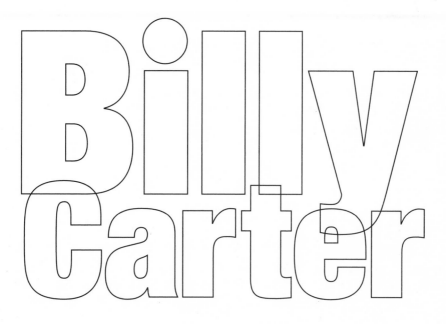

Billy Carter

A Journey Through the Shadows

WILLIAM "BUDDY" CARTER

LONGSTREET
Atlanta, Georgia

Published by
LONGSTREET, INC.
A subsidiary of Cox Newspapers
A subsidiary of Cox Enterprises, Inc.
2140 Newmarket Parkway
Suite 122
Marietta, GA 30067

Printed in the United States of America

1st printing 1999

Library of Congress Catalog Card Number: 99-61751

ISBN: 1-56352-553-4

Jacket and book design by Burtch Hunter

Visit Longstreet on the World Wide Web
WWW.LSPRESS.COM

For Mama

*"Serenity is not freedom from the storm—
but peace amid the storm."*

Billy Carter

Chapter One

I was laughing when the hearse backed into Mama's driveway.

I was laughing and so were the three or four men standing with me beneath the carport. We were all dressed up in dark blue suits and ties and good, solid Sunday shoes. I remember wiping sweat from my forehead with the sleeve of my suit coat because it was mid-September in south Georgia; fine, fall weather for most other parts of the country but still hotter than hell in Plains.

But the heat didn't really bother me or the men I was standing with. We'd grown up with it; lived with it all our lives. And the laughter kept our minds from the gnats and the humidity and the reason we were clustered together under the carport.

I don't remember the particular story we were laughing about. It didn't really matter. There were so many myths and legends and "so-help-me-God, right-hand-'fore-Jesus, he really did this" stories about my old man, I truly believe we could have stood in that one spot for three days, remembering and remembering, and still had a few more to tell.

But then the hearse from Hancock Funeral Home kind of

floated in and the true, loud laughter turned nervous before dying away completely.

Mama's yard is a carpet of thick, dark green centipede bordered with eight- and twelve-foot camellias and four or five different varieties of azalea. There is a fairly good-sized pecan tree in the middle along with a pine or two. Scattered about that carpet, beneath the shade of the trees, stood several different groups of people clustered together in knots. Each knot was protected by a barrier of sorts made evident by the clothes they wore or by the way they stood or by the way they looked around to see who was looking at them.

I caught glimpses of faces I almost knew but couldn't quite put names to. Faces that had played parts, good or bad, in my old man's life. Some faces I knew as well as my own. I remember looking at some of these people and wondering what the hell they were doing there. There were a few, I know, who showed up only to make sure he was dead.

There were cliques of Atlanta folk, 120 miles south from the protection of tall buildings and the myth of Tara, who stood together whispering politely, seemingly bemused at the clouds of gnats boiling about their faces and at the light haze of red dust hanging in the air. Some were distant kin; the kind who show up only for weddings or funerals. A few were old friends. Most, but definitely not all, of the Atlanta crowd came out of courtesy to my uncle.

Tourists walked from downtown to Mama's yard and stood gaping with that particular tourist look on their faces and cameras in their hands. I was a little irritated at this intrusion but didn't want to run anyone away, didn't want to cause a scene. I wanted to think maybe some of the tourists were there out of respect for my dad. But then I remembered my grandmother's funeral, a few years before, when people no one in the family knew came into her home and took flowers from the arrangements and from the blanket of white roses covering her coffin. How could these people even think we would want them there?

But the thing is, they *were* there. And they were there in the beginning, when my father's life became public. They came to Plains and sought him out, listened to his stories and his bullshit and laughed with him. Got their pictures taken standing beside him; him with a beer in his hand and a grin on his face. Many times, holding tightly to his hand, these people would lean in, after looking around to see if anyone was listening, to whisper to my old man that they wished *he* had run for president. "Hell, you're one of us," they would say. "You got *common sense*." And he would always leave them with something they could go back and tell their friends about. Maybe something a little profane or something funny. But he always left them with a Billy story to tell. Then all the trouble started and they were still there, telling him to hang on, not to give up. A bit proud, maybe, in some weird way, that this man, this celebrity of sorts, had problems, too.

I couldn't help thinking then that the old man might have been comforted to know these folks had made a trek to Plains to see him on his way. That some of the ones who supported him and loved him in the beginning still thought kindly of him in the end. I found myself glad they were there.

Part of what drew the tourists was the mass of reporters and camera people across the street from Mama's house. Every so often a man my father never cared for would cross 280 and speak for a few minutes with the press. He'd appointed himself "family spokesman," something that infuriated my mother, my sisters and me. It seemed that so often in the past few years someone was claiming the right to speak for my dad, as if he, or one of us, were too feeble-minded to do it ourselves. I often thought of these "spokesmen" as part of some secret damage-control or PR team put together to keep the Carter image dust-free and brightly shined.

Some of the press, I'm sure, came expecting to see the old man laid to rest sitting upright in a pink Cadillac with a beer in his hand and a cigarette in his mouth. Maybe he'd be led to Lebanon Cemetery by a pack of coon-dogs or a gang of over-all-clad, good-'ol-boys, yee-hawing and firing guns in the air. This would not have been at all out of character with some of the things I'd seen written about him while he was living and, in truth, I was a little surprised at the respect with which he was treated by the press in death.

Most of the reporters were kept away, across the street. Others, who had become our friends, became part of our family, came without their trade tools to genuinely join in the mourning and the remembering. Like those of us who'd been around my dad for most of his life, they knew a different Billy from the rest of the world.

At first glance, I thought most of those in Mama's yard were people my dad barely knew; outsiders who were there because they felt they *had* to be. But then people kept coming and the yard filled with those who *wanted* to be there, who wanted me and Mama and my sisters and brother to know we weren't alone; we weren't the only ones with big, giant holes in our hearts. There were farmers, just an hour or so out of the fields, who shut down their machines to clean up and come and pat Mama's hands with theirs and cry, as much as these men do, at the passing of one of their own. They stood together, shy and self-conscious, a little uncomfortable in the suits they rarely wore outside of Sunday. A good bit of the population of Plains had showed up; both black and white. Everyone had interacted in some form or fashion with my old man in the fifty-one years he was around. They'd either worked for him or with him. Or against him. Some had been pissed off with him at one time or another. He'd been pissed at them. Some had drunk gallons of beer and bourbon with him, won his money at poker, got him in trouble with Mama or rode miles and miles and miles of red dirt roads with him. At times, he'd given what was his to some of these people who, in turn, gave back to him when he was in need. There seemed to be a million old ladies there who were real old when I was young and who I'm sure had whipped Daddy's ass or wiped his nose when he was a kid. A few of the folks had last seen him when he was healthy and full of fire and now seemed a bit stunned he wasn't out in the yard with them, telling lies.

And everybody had something to say; some story to tell. Something to laugh about. To tell the truth, we were all having a good time out there in Mama's yard. Until that goddamned hearse pulled up.

I don't remember if any of my sisters or my brother were out there with me. At that moment it seemed as if I were the only one in the world standing beneath the carport. There certainly was no noise; everyone had become silent. Everyone, I felt, was staring at me.

I walked to the back of the hearse and looked through one of the small windows. I don't know why. I knew he was in there, laid out in that cherry coffin, dressed in a pair of cowboy boots, blue jeans, a Tom T. Hall concert T-shirt and a peach-colored sports coat given to him by Leon Johnson, one of his cronies. This is what I'd been told, at least. I hadn't actually seen him since he'd been taken from the house the morning before. Mama and my sisters had all driven the nine miles to Americus to see him after Hancock's had finished their job. Even my little brother, who was twelve, went to see him one last time. "He looked good. He looked real good," they all said. "You should have gone to see him, Buddy, he looked like he was well."

I know why Mama went. She'd spent the last thirty-three years taking care of him and was going to make damned sure they took care of him now. My sisters and my brother went to make sure, too. And I imagine they took his hand or patted his face and cried beside him before the coffin was closed. Sometimes I wonder if I should have taken my last chance to look upon him. I wonder if I would have thought he looked good, too. But I know I wouldn't have. I would've seen my old man lying there and thought about him being dead, no matter how good he looked. And I'm glad I didn't. I'm glad I said good-bye the last night he was alive and in his own room at home. Because now, when I think of him, I think of him living.

The weight of a hand upon my shoulder drew my eyes from that cherry coffin, and the man from the funeral home said something to me, though I don't know what. All I could think about was going inside and telling Mama that Daddy was here; he was ready to go.

A few more people patted my back and spoke to me as I walked into the house. I looked for Mama in the living room but couldn't see her for the crowd. There seemed to be as many people inside as out. I moved through, speaking and being spoken to, and was taken a bit by surprise to see two people I didn't know sitting in my folks' side-by-side easy chairs. They shouldn't have been there. *Nobody* sat in the old man's chair. I moved away, a little worried, looking for my mother. I hoped she wasn't in the kitchen trying to cook for all these people. The most natural thing in the world would be for her to be in there fixing iced tea and checking the corn-bread in the oven. She needed to take care of folks.

A lady I'd known all my life stopped me and asked if I'd eaten. "You gotta eat, hon," she said, and put a plate in my hands. I thanked her and wondered how long she and the other ladies had been there. I know that within an hour after my dad died, early in the morning before, she and a few more had showed up. They all had food, of course. And they began cleaning the house and washing clothes and laying the table in preparation for the crowd. Never intruding, but always there with a cup of coffee or a gentle scolding to get some rest. I've not been to many funerals in my life, and all of those have been here, in my hometown, but these women were always there, doing what they were doing now. And I wondered how it was these beautiful ladies found their way to the homes of those in need. Was there some kind of network? Did they somehow sense one less soul populating Plains? I took a bite of food and the lady smiled at me.

I found Mama in the dining room. She looked unnatural and out of place to me, sitting there in a straight-back chair in the corner beside the china cabinet. She was dressed in black and trying hard to smile at all the people who'd come to speak with Miss Sybil. And though I could tell she was a little confused, a bit afraid, she still made every one of these people feel welcomed into her home as if they'd just dropped by for an afternoon visit. She was tired, I knew, from spending the last year no more than a few steps away from my father and from helping him breathe his last breaths less than a day and a half before. Maybe, too, she was thinking of the days, the years, ahead. I'd been amazed at how she'd held up. But from the look in her eyes now I could tell she wanted to go away; to be alone for a while. Maybe to just *be* alone. Maybe to scream. And knowing all the while she sat in that chair, smiling at folks and comforting them, that she couldn't. Not for a while, at least. Things had moved a lot faster than any of us had expected since the morning before. Normally when a person dies—in Plains, at least—there is a day between the death and the funeral to allow traveling time for out-of-towners and a little room for the family to face what has happened. But someone came to my mother on the day of my father's death and asked her if there was any reason to wait for the burial. "The President is leaving for Africa the day after tomorrow," they said. So Daddy was buried a day early. I've often thought that whoever my uncle was going to see would have given him a day of grace if he'd only asked for it; given him a day to bury his brother. Instead, it became just another concession made. The last in a long line, I hoped. Mama told me later she didn't like the idea but didn't want to "be ugly" about it.

I didn't like it either, but there wasn't much I could do about it. So the night before the funeral I got drunk and, with my sisters and brother, taped together four or five bedsheets and painted upon it: *PLAINS GEORGIA HOME OF BILLY CARTER. We love you*, it said at the bottom. And we all signed our names to it. Downtown, on Main Street, above the old Carter's Warehouse office, is a huge sign proclaiming Plains to be the home of Jimmy Carter—*Our 39th President*. The sign had been painted and installed when my uncle ran for governor and won. It was payment on a bet my dad had made with him. If you win, he said, I'll pay to have a sign put up. It had been there ever since; changing in 1976 and now touched up from time to time. I still can't say why I, along with my brother-in-law, climbed up there and furiously stapled those sheets to that painted plywood. Except that it made me feel better. And it was probably the drunk thing to do. Maybe it was a way to tell the world my dad lived here, too. He counted. That he wasn't quite the screw-up some people made him out to be. Because we loved him and put up a painted bedsheet that said so. If he'd been alive, I think he would have kicked my ass. But it would have been worth it.

There was a crowd around Mama and I eased my way through to tell her it was time. "Where's Earl?" she asked, looking to me to find my little brother. He and my youngest sister, Mandy, had been the only two of us six children living at home during the last year of my dad's life. But Mandy was working for the *Americus Times-Recorder* and had a way to take her mind, a few hours a day, off of the cloud floating around my parents' house. The rest of us were married and had families of our own. Earl, though, was witness to it all. Years later I asked him what it was like. "Weird," he said. I don't think he knew then what a comfort he was to my old man and my mother. And I don't think I would have traded places with him for anything in the world. I found him and we all prepared to leave.

I don't remember who was in the car with me except for my wife, Marlene. I do remember the barely more than a mile ride to Lebanon Cemetery seeming to last days and days. And I wish we were still riding, because I knew when we stopped, it would be the end. We rode west on 280, past peanut fields, bare of harvest now, waiting to be turned. We rode past groves of pine. We rode past homes of those who'd been part of my dad's life, homes of those who'd taken the trip he was taking now, homes of those who would ride this ride in the future. I thought about the thousands and thousands of times the old man had driven this road himself, either on his way to the Pond House, where my grandmother lived, or a few yards further to take a right on Rabbit Branch Road which led to some of the dirt roads of Sumter County he loved to prowl. We took a left onto an unlined, black-top road that, if we'd kept going, would have ended up at his boyhood home. So close, I thought. So close to the beginning of his life. Maybe if we'd kept going we could have started all over again.

Both sides of the road were lined with cars, a quarter-mile from the cemetery, and a loose crowd of people, dressed in their best, was making its way up the hill. Again, I saw those I'd known all my life, some just this side of familiar, some I didn't know at all. I felt I should wave but didn't. And then we took that last right turn.

My great-uncle Buddy was buried there not far from his brother, the grandfather I never knew. My grandma, Miss Lillian, was there, too, as well and my granddaddy and granny, my mother's folks. If I didn't know all the people buried there, I at least knew their names. They were part of the world I'd wandered through as a child. They were the reason I was me. Lebanon Cemetery is not really a welcoming place. Most of the stones are a weathered gray, framed by weeds or wildflowers struggling to live through hard-packed clay. It is bare of trees and wide open to the south Georgia sun. There are red-ant hills and lizards and always, to me, at least, the feeling that some discontented spirit was watching from the woods. But in spite of this, the trips I'd taken there, alone, had always left me with a feeling of comfort; I knew there was always a place, if I chose it, for me to go when my end had come.

And then we stopped and there was the confusion of where to sit and what to do. We were led to the chairs reserved for family, facing the open grave. There was a pile of dirt covered with green astroturf and we sat beneath a tent of the same color. There were piles and piles of flowers and there were hundreds of people talking low or whispering. And then some of my father's buddies brought that cherry coffin from the hearse and put it before us. I think this is when I knew it all was true.

Then the whispering and the rustling from the crowd around us stopped when Tom T., my father's friend, stepped up beside my dad and began to speak. "Brother Bill," he said, "is being buried without a tie. The family would like for all the gentlemen here to honor him by removing theirs." And I looked around at all the faces and saw most of them grinning as they tugged the ties from around their necks. I caught a grimace or two from some who didn't know my dad that well at what they thought of as a breach of protocol. But I liked it.

And Tom said, "Lord, when we turn our hand to such tasks as eulogizing our brother, we find ourselves frustrated with convention. We so cherish this brotherhood that we might make more of it than you intended.

"Lord, we have to wonder if Billy Carter was the good old boy that he was reported to be. Billy was not always good, and he was the first to admit it. He was not old and never lived to be, and he most certainly was not a boy. Billy Carter was a man.

"When a poet friend learned that Billy Carter was faced with his dread disease, he asked, 'How will he die?'

"Lord, let us report in your presence that he died with courage. And that is not to say that he went gently into that good night."

As I sat and listened to the words this man had written about my father, as rapt as most of those around me, I began to realize my old man was much more than the person I had butted heads with throughout the years. More than the man I had feared at times; had hated at others. More than the man I'd admired and respected and loved. He'd been a lot more. And as I listened, all I could think about was how I'd never taken the time, as none of us had, really, to tell him what he'd meant to most of us here.

"Lord, let us go back to a summer's day of a few months ago when the sun was shining on this beautiful Georgia country-side. Let us hear the laughter of Billy Carter and see that smile . . . and that alone will help us make it through this day.

"Lord, we are thankful for Sybil Carter and these beautiful children and grandchildren. We are witness to the wisdom that you have given them the charms and sensibilities that we so admired in our departed friend.

"We are grateful for the friends and family of Billy Carter. Their vast number signals the courage, the strength and the vehicle by which we can carry his memory into the future.

"Lord, if in our zeal to keep our good friend so long with us, we fail to admit to the realities of which we are so often and so brutally reminded, please accept that we loved this man who never gave up on us, and accept that we cannot so readily give up on him.

"We cannot bring ourselves to say that we have lost a friend. We are of the opinion that we have lost *the* friend. The only friend who was just like this. So special, so kind, so good and so unlikely to be a victim of such raw and unreasonable a fate.

"But take him Lord, this worn body. Please leave us the memory of his laughter, his smile, his caring and all that we knew and loved of him . . . leave that without which we would be so much the poorer.

"Amen."

After that, there was not much left to say. Brother Will Campbell said a few words and Reverend Dan Arial spoke for a minute or two. And less than thirty minutes after my old man's last ride, we left him there and went back to Mama's house.

The same crowd was there, but this time a little more relaxed than an hour before. A lot of food was eaten and there was more of a party atmosphere. I think Daddy would have liked that. And the stories and the laughter began again, just like they always do when any of us get together. I hugged my sisters a lot afterwards. We'd pass each other in the yard or in the house and hug each other and cry a little bit. And Mama. God, it's a wonder she wasn't bruised and battered as much as we held onto her that day.

And then the crowd got to me and I had to find a place to

hide. I found myself in the backyard, sitting beneath the gazebo. I'd gone there early the morning before, an hour or so after Daddy had died. I looked for signs that morning, as I think we all do, of his passing. A breeze where there had been none, maybe, or a hawk flying way up in the sky. Something, anything, to bid us all good-bye or to announce his arrival to the other side.

I began to laugh at myself, expecting such gentle acts from my old man. There'd be no birds or breezes from Billy Carter.

Hell no.

He'd need a hurricane.

Someone asked me one time to think about how it would have been if I'd had a "normal" childhood. What if, for instance, my father had taken the time to play baseball with me or taught me how to hunt? How different would your life be now? I was asked. My oldest sister Kim was with me at the time, and both of us laughed at the thought of Billy Carter participating in any kind of organized family activity. It's just not something he did and we never expected him to. My father was much different around us, the family, from the way he was with his friends or the public in general. He thought of us as his possessions. We were easy to ignore as long as we did what we were told. And we always did what we were told because the combination of the old man's Carter hard-headedness and his alcoholism was a horrible thing to behold, and we did what we could to keep it quiet. This is not to say we had terrible childhoods; we didn't. As a matter of fact, I think I had one of the best times growing up that a kid could have. Most of what my sisters and I knew about my dad were his moods and his alcoholism and we just lived with them. And we loved him.

So the first memories I have of my old man are not of hazy, summer afternoons with him grilling in the backyard and playing tag with us kids. There were never any long walks, him with his arm around my shoulder, or long father/son talks about things. No, my first memories of my old man aren't the ones I imagine other people have of their fathers. And I've become suspicious of those who claim to recall entire conversations and feelings from when they were three or four years old. I only remember snatches of things from when I was that age. My very first memory is of my granny. She is sitting outside in a green, metal lawn chair. It is hot and I am wearing shorts. Granny is wearing a cotton, print dress and an apron. Between her legs is a white, enameled dishpan with a red stripe around the rim, filled with butter beans. She is shelling them with a speed I still find phenomenal and getting on my ass about something. I think the intensity of the situation left an imprint: the sun on my bare back, the sweat on my face, the smell of summer and granddaddy's garden, and the terror at getting caught doing something I wasn't supposed to by someone I loved. It is very vivid for me and very much unlike my first memory of my father, which is of him walking. Walking with his head down, in a lumbering, arm-swinging, slow-moving gait, the ever-present, nonfiltered Pall Mall in his left hand. And his shoulders were slumped, always slumped, as if somehow he was testing the weight of things to come. And I remember the sighs, too. The sighs that spoke more than any words he could have uttered. Sometimes I think he became weary of the world much earlier than most and much more than many.

But, of course, at that age I wasn't yet aware of any of this. My goals then were no further than what I could see. My goal was to do whatever had to be done in my little kid world. And my little kid world was Plains, one hell of a place to be.

Rural Georgia in the sixties was still decades away from catching up with the rest of the country. And the Plains I grew up in, the one not yet tainted by tourists or looked upon by the eyes of the world, is not there anymore. Maybe it never really was. Because the Plains I grew up in, I admit, has become almost mythical for me. A place I can never have back. But for a few years, at least, the years I like to think of as the ones that made me who I am, I lived in the best place in the world.

Our house was at the end of Bond Street on the north side of town. It was big and rambling and old and sat on a three-quarter acre lot bordering a peanut field. There was a huge pecan tree in front and one in back with a treehouse. The back fence was covered in summer with honeysuckle vine and at one end of the fencerow was a big tangle of forsythia, perfect for tunneling and hiding in. We had a barn/shed-type building that at different times housed a horse named Ace, two bird dogs who wouldn't eat my sister's homemade jelly rolls, and a billy goat named Mac my dad sneaked in as a pet for us kids. We tried to keep him hidden from our mother, but after only one day the smell busted his cover and we had to get rid of him. Mama ruled in such matters. Behind the barn we had the Bat-Man club, which was nothing more than a crude pair of wings painted on the planks with our names, mine and my oldest sister's, painted beneath them. It was all designed only to aggravate and exclude our sister Jana.

The house is wooden clapboard supported by brick. Beneath the house it was always cool and dark and scary, but a wonderful place to hide. You could lie there, in the dusty dark, and listen to the muffled voices from the TV or from the family and follow them from room to room by the sound of their footsteps across the wooden floor. Sheba, our family dog, had her puppies in one far, dark corner, the one place I never dared to explore, and I remember how her eyes glowed green from the flashlight my dad used to find her. Buried beneath the house still, I hope, are untold treasures, safe in tin cracker boxes and cushioned with cotton: green army men with plastic parachutes, dog-eared baseball cards, foreign coins, a pocket knife or two, and a fortune, *a fortune,* in pennies. It was a place of refuge for me there beneath the house, and where I fled to when I burnt the barn, badly mistaken that no one would follow. No one except my dad. And though I was scrunched back as far as I could go, he came in after me. I remember being amazed amidst my terror at how he kept coming. My belly was pressed hard to the dirt and the floor beams were mere inches above my back. But like some early version of the Terminator, my old man kept coming. I don't remember how badly he beat my ass when he finally dragged me out; I deserved it.

The driveway was dirt and I remember my mother showing us how to draw our own houses with sticks fallen from the pecan tree. We drew room after room and sat among them, in the dust, daring anyone to cross the lines. In the fall, that same tree dropped what seemed to be a million pecans. My sister Jana and I, the undisputed troublemakers, were often banished to the yard, as punishment, to pick them up. I remember sitting there with her, in a huge pile of leaves, with snot running down our faces, as we planned to run away forever. They'd be sorry, we knew, for forcing us into hard labor on cool, autumn afternoons. The pain was always eased, though, when Daddy would sell the pecans in Americus and give us the money to buy Christmas presents for each other. The leaves from the tree were raked to the ditch in the front yard and burned. And we'd stand around the pile for hours, poking at the fire with sticks. That smell of burning leaves was like a perfume and reminded us that Halloween was just a few short weeks away.

We always entered the house from the back door, never the front, and into the den. There were two easy chairs, one for my mother and one for my father, and a sofa between them. A big, wagon-wheel coffee table took up most of the middle, and there were books everywhere. The floor was carpeted in a rust-colored shag and against one wall was a console, color TV. I spent many Saturday mornings lounging on the floor watching Spider Man cartoons and trying to avoid getting beat up by my sister Jana, who we—me and my other sisters—called "Tank." Around about eleven o'clock, "Ridley Bell's Sportsman's Lodge," sponsored by RC Cola, would come on and it was time to turn the TV over to the grown-ups and go outside. Most Saturday and Sunday afternoons, if he was back from cruising with his buddies or it wasn't peanut season, the den belonged to the old man; it was his domain. He'd lay on the sofa, in his Bermuda shorts, with a book in front of his face and a ball game on TV. Invariably he fell asleep while Mama spent the afternoon constantly shushing us and warning against waking Daddy up. And as bad as it was for us if we did, we always found some reason to tiptoe into the den to look at him, as if he were a sleeping dragon or some forbidden thing. There was a delicious fear there and well worth, I think, waking him up only to be glared upon or barked at.

I remember what seems to be a hundred Christmas mornings in the den around a cut cedar that never seemed to stand straight. It dripped with clumps of tinsel and shined with big bulbs. Three or four of the ornaments had belonged to my Granny. Inside the ornaments was a pinwheel of foil that spun from the heat of the lights. For a few weeks after the tree was removed, bare feet were pricked by dried needles of cedar clinging to the carpet.

My new baby sister was brought into our lives through the door of the den. Several local teenage boys came through there, too, nervous to the point of speechlessness, to fidget on the sofa before meeting my dad; a requirement to dating my oldest sister. And on the wall beside the door to the den was the double window my father, in a fit of rage over some imagined thing, hurled the telephone through after ripping it from the wall. We were forbidden to pick up the glass or touch the phone, which lay in the yard for two days.

The door from the den led to the kitchen. To the right was the dining area. Anyone coming into our home during mealtimes would, of course, be invited to the table and given a heaped plate. But conversation was out of the question because all of us—my folks, my sisters and I—read during meals. Our faces were obscured by paperbacks, and the clink of stainless steel on china would be accompanied by the whisk of pages being turned. Definitely not a Norman Rockwell setting and something we never carried into other people's homes. I, at least, have continued this guilty pleasure, because it is almost impossible for me to enjoy a meal now without the help of Stephen King or James Lee Burke. We all had to wait for my old man to come home and shower before we ate supper; sometimes very late, because, though he rarely spoke during that meal, he insisted we all be there.

I remember one Sunday morning, with the newspaper scattered all around the table, when I declared myself finished eating. The old man peered over the top of his folded page to look at my plate. "Eat the eggs," he commanded and disappeared again into the news. The eggs were scrambled and I would rather eat bugs. But *he* had spoken, our god, and my sister Kim, who sat beside me, knew it. I could hear evil snickers from behind the cover of a Bobbsey Twins adventure and then her hand snaked up to grasp the glass of water beside her plate. I watched in horror as she poured the water over my eggs. They floated there, mingling with the remnants of my breakfast: bits of toast and bacon, grape jelly and grits. It was an evil beyond evil and, of course, I told on her. And, of course, the old man made her eat it. Sweet.

The kitchen was pretty big and the hub of the house. All the birthday cakes were baked there; some by my sister Jana who seemed to always, in her excitement, forget how to spell. Most of us, at one time or another, were presented with one of her lopsided cakes declaring "Happy Brithday" across the top in frosting. And I remember cool winter mornings standing around the open oven door, warming up, while Mama made cheese toast. Just off the kitchen was a small room with a washer, a dryer, and a big chest freezer. Johnnie Mae Streeter, the black lady who helped Mama with the house and us six kids, would stand in front of the freezer while she ironed, watching her "stories" on the small black-and-white TV that sat on top.

The door from the kitchen led to my sister Marle's room. It had once been the living room before the other was added. In one corner, the hardwood floor is splintered and scarred from the force of a hoe my old man used to chop up a rat snake that decided to visit. A big, gas heater stood in front of the fireplace and, wherever it is now, still holds traces of skin from my behind from when I backed up too close after a bath one winter's night.

Next to Marle's was what was once a storage room and forbidden to us kids. Later, it became my oldest sister's room. The rest of us were jealous of her privacy and would gather around the closed door, listening and giggling, at her attempts to sing along with the record player.

The other door from Marle's room led to the middle of the house, a big room I imagine was once the center of activity. There were six doors that opened up into other rooms from this one. For years, this was my room. There was constant traffic from my folks and my sisters passing through to get to their own rooms.

Before that, I slept in a room off the central one. It was tiny and had no windows. And I remember lying there, wide awake, in that little, dark room listening to the murmur of the old man's radio, which he kept on all night. Baseball, mostly, out of Atlanta. But some nights, way past the time I should have lost the battle with sleep, I could hear the sound of a creaking door followed by the deep voice of a man speaking, announcing the beginning of a radio show. The words were never clear to me, but I could hear the tinny sounds of serious conversations, footsteps and, sometimes, gunfire. And I would close my eyes tightly, because somehow, the darkness behind my eyelids seemed so much brighter than the blackness of my room.

Another door led to Jana's room, where she swears she woke one night to see the devil sitting cross-legged in front of the gas heater, grinning at her. The walls were once covered with Donnie Osmond posters, but beyond that I don't remember much. The rest of us were pretty much terrified of her, and getting caught in her room meant a guaranteed ass-beating.

And then there was my folks' room; a forbidden, secret place that smelled of Mama's Saturday-night-going-out-dancing perfume. I remember creeping in to peek at my new baby sister Mandy in her crib. This was after I'd gotten over being upset at having another girl to contend with. Behind the door was a rack of leather belts, most of which had met the backs of my legs at one time or another. Half the punishment was watching my father choose which one to use. He'd put his hand on one, then pause, as if reconsidering, then move to another. There were always a few seconds when I dared hope for a reprieve. I don't remember it ever happening, though.

The room at the front of the house was formal and we rarely went in there. It, too, was once the living room where we all watched TV. It's where I witnessed the moon landing. I sat there, late at night, a skinheaded, vacant-eyed and drooling nine-year-old; jerking awake every time the old man would bark out, "Wake up! You need to see this!" I don't think I've ever recovered from that lack of sleep.

My memories of that house are as vivid to me as if they were pictures in a book. The good ones are as good as can be. Most of the bad ones seem to be made up of Mama as mediator; the great protector, while the old man comes through— not always, but a good bit of the time—as some kind of all-powerful shadow. A shadow we avoided if we could. It's not as if he lurched through the house in a rage, intent on terrifying us. Most of the time he sat silently and ticked, a ticking tempered by his disease. And during those times we tiptoed our way around him; avoiding eye contact and trying to do right as far as he saw it or hoping one of his better moods would somehow surface. We all became masters at reading his face and would peer out the window when he came home; we were able to divine whether or not to scatter to our rooms or stay in his presence, where we really all wanted to be. There were plenty of good times in that house with my father—plenty. But, even as a kid, I had the feeling those times were somehow brittle; apt to crash and fall without warning.

The house still stands, though another family lives there now. And I've wondered a lot if bits of us still live there, too. I think so, because on my trips back to Plains, as I cruise the old roads, I slow down as I pass. Maybe expecting to see myself sitting in the dirt of the driveway, screaming bloody murder as Tank tries to intrude in my make-believe rooms. And I still laugh when I look at the barn, knowing that buried deep behind it is a Barbie Dream House in pieces; a well-intentioned project never completed by my old man and my granddaddy after a meeting with Jim Beam late one Christmas Eve. And it is a comfort to know that in one shady corner, beneath a chinaberry tree, our dog Sheba rests next to Mr. Bud, a mutt who could sing.

I look at Plains itself as an extension of the house. There was never a question as to whether or not a kid should play in the yard or wander around town. We were all protected by the fact that Plains was Plains; a farming community of 750 people nine miles from nowhere. A quarter-mile north of our house the blacktop abruptly ended at the beginning of a red dirt road that led to deep groves of pine; wide open fields; fat, wild plums and great adventures. Across from the southeast corner of our yard, where the road splits, is a stone road marker in the shape of a cross. Etched on the stone are the legends: *Kidd's Mill* and *Magnolia Springs*, with two arrows pointing to the left. I always thought of that marker as the end of town, because a few hundred feet south of our yard the sidewalk began and the heart of town was only a slow, ten-minute walk away.

The sidewalk began at the corner of our next-door neighbor's yard. Mr. Guy lived in a small, white clapboard house, and for years I was in awe of him as the man in charge of the candy counter at the Plains Mercantile. He did other things, I'm sure, but I always remember him as the tall, thin man in green work clothes who stood patiently waiting for me to choose from the stupefying selection behind the glass. There was a narrow dirt road beside his house that was our shortcut to the Lion's Club swimming pool. The road was bordered on both sides by rusted wire fences covered in a tangle of wild blackberry. The walk to the pool was always a fast one, anticipating a day of fun. I'm surprised now at how small the pool is. Then, it seemed to be a mile across and a hundred yards deep. Inside the chain-link fence surrounding the pool is a wide border of grass dotted with mimosa trees and round, concrete picnic tables. There's a small, brick-o-block concession stand flanked by dressing rooms. The dressing rooms had drains in the floor and always smelled strongly of pee and chlorine. There always seemed to be a hundred people there, screaming and splashing and lying in the sun. The walk back home started out fast, too, with a few hundred yards of blacktop burning our feet before reaching our shortcut. Then we ambled down our dirt road, exhausted and sunburnt, reviving ourselves with a sugar rush of Zero candy bars and giant Pixie sticks bought from the concession stand.

The walk downtown from our house led past two churches, the Baptist and the Lutheran, and was shaded in places by crepe myrtle and magnolia trees. I always walked on one side of Bond Street going down and the other coming home. A ritual I followed without fail and one I've yet to figure out. Plains High School took up most of one side of the street with its ball field and outbuildings. I spent my first two years of school there before integration, when I was moved to Westside Elementary to begin third grade. The big, metal gymnasium is gone now and the main building of the old high school is a museum. Part of the pleasure of the walk was passing Miss Anne's, a lady who could make things grow just by looking at them. She always seemed to be out in her yard with a small pair of pruners or a trowel in her hand as if she herself had somehow sprung from the soil. At the end of the sidewalk was Highway 280. Across 280 was the railroad tracks and Main Street and downtown Plains.

When I was a child, this town of 750 souls supported two grocery stores, a drug store, a mercantile, two gas stations, a barber shop, a bank and a honky-tonk or two. And, of course, several churches. Main Street Plains has always reminded me of a movie set. The storefronts are two-story brick with wide plate-glass windows and heavy wood-framed doors. The sidewalks are shaded from the sun with a tin awning supported by wooden posts. The stores are deeper than they are wide and floored with hardwood or heavy ceramic tile. Every day there were people on the sidewalks, moving in and out of the stores, conducting business, and Saturday nights were almost carnival-like. Tractors were as common as cars on the streets and, depending on the season, big metal or wooden wagons, filled with peanuts or corn or cotton, rumbled up and down 280 or Highway 45 to turn into one of the two warehouse businesses in town: Plains Cotton Warehouse, owned by the Williams family, or Carter's Warehouse, belonging to my family.

Sometimes the air would be filled, like snow, with tiny bits of cotton from the gin, and on August and September nights, after the sounds of the town had died, the faint roar of peanut dryers lulled you to sleep. In the middle of town stood the water tower; a huge, silver, "War of the Worlds" martian, flecked with rust. My sister Jana and I once tried to fly from its side, from a few rungs up, on wings made of newspaper. And I am told my father and my uncle once fist-fought beneath the tower, in full view of the town, shaming my grandmother. A few steps from the tower, back across 280, was Mr. Mill's gas station, the one my father later bought in 1972. By day, Mr. Mill's was your standard full-service filling station, and you could see him darting about in his tan work uniform, his hair shockingly white, pumping gas, checking oil and fixing tires. When the evening came, though, the old, wooden theater seats along one outside wall of the station filled with men doing men things and, it was rumored, drinking beer.

At any time, on any day but Sunday, three or four people

could be seen in front of the post office, collecting a dose of daily gossip to carry home to their families. Men gathered around the backs of pick-up trucks to lean on the bed or prop one foot on the bumper, sweat-stained and dust-covered, to discuss farming or feeding or things best left for men to discuss. For years I thought every farmer in town carried with them, in the beds of their trucks, amazing and wonderful things only grown-ups were allowed to look upon. Years later I learned there was nothing much to see: tractor parts, empty beer bottles, bags of feed or fertilizer, clusters of peanuts on dried vines where the crop had been checked. But I now know, if I could have seen them, the beds of those trucks would have been overflowing with a million stories or more.

From the heart of town, it was only a few minutes walk in any direction to any one of my favorite places. My granny and granddaddy's house, where granddaddy sometimes kept caged raccoons on his front porch and whose yard was the best place in south Georgia to catch lightning bugs. My grandma's house, where my cousin Michael and I would fight over the window seat in the built-in breakfast nook in the kitchen and where, when the attic fan was turned on to cool the house, you could blow up balloons and watch them drift slowly through the house and up the stairs to enter the attic door, then stick to the wire grate covering the giant blades. The woods and what all the kids called the "bottle graveyard," the long-abandoned town dump where, beneath years and years of fallen leaves, you could dig and scratch and come up with all kinds of surprises only those of certain ages could appreciate.

Most of the buildings on Main Street are empty now. No more groceries or hardware are sold from the stores. The candy counter is gone as well as the barber shop, and Plains Mercantile has long since closed. There are a few shelves of dusty, plastic things stamped with my uncle's name that the tourists, more often than not, pick up to look at, then put down again. There are clumps of weeds poking through the concrete parking lot of Mr. Mill's gas station and the shed over the rack has collapsed. Saturday nights are as dead now as Monday mornings, and trading is done nine miles away, in Americus, at the big discount places.

But as empty as my town may seem now, it is still filled with ghosts. And the ghosts of all those familiar things still flit about. Especially in summer, on twilight walks, when the air is filled with brown beetles and the creak of porch swings. It's as if in the quiet of night Plains goes back to how it used to be. Or we can at least pretend it has. And then those old ghosts are welcomed.

Sometimes, on visits home, it seems as though the ghosts have spent their time waiting for me and are eager to be seen. The old man, especially, waits. He is in my mother's home, watching over her and standing around the bed of every pick-up truck I see. And I imagine I see him walking sometimes, with his shoulders slumped, along the streets of Plains. But most of all I see him when I ride the old roads, from the corner of my eye; as if he sits beside me.

That is where the old man and I began, riding.

By the time I was born, my parents already had two daughters, Kim and Jana. To prove he was capable of fathering a son, I am told, only four days after I was born my dad put me in the front of his truck with him and drove me around town showing me to his friends. My dad's friends, being who they were and knowing him, made him prove I was a boy by unpinning my diaper and exposing me to the world. This was my initiation, so to speak, into my father's secret world of riding. It was a man thing.

The rides were an escape for him, I think, and the hundreds of miles of dirt roads, field trails, and unlined county blacktop were safe. He and Bud Duvall, his best friend from childhood, knew every farm, every abandoned shack, every beaver pond, and every pine grove in Sumter and Webster counties. Sometimes, when I'd been invited to ride, he would ask, after an hour or two of driving, "Do you know where you are?" I never did, because it was a point of pride for him to get me, or one of his buddies, lost. More often than not, we were five miles or less from Plains on some road that could have been in Michigan as far as I knew. I don't think there's anybody who would dispute the fact that he knew the roads around home better than anyone.

And riding was part of his job. Riding and visiting. My family was in the agricultural business. We bought crops from farmers and sold them to various processors. The farmers, in turn, bought seed, fertilizer, pesticides and herbicides from us. We depended on the farmers as much as the farmers depended on the weather. Bad times for the farmers meant bad times for Plains. When planting or harvesting times came around, it was not unusual for my old man to leave the house at four-thirty in the morning, no later than five, to begin his rounds. He met farmers in the field, if only for a word or two; others waved in passing. Some told him what would be needed later in the day or week as far as chemicals or supplies were concerned. Most of these men barely had time to eat during peak season, much less the time to place orders over the phone. He rode again late in the afternoon and sometimes at night, checking on the farmers and the fields. It's not something that was demanded of him. He loved it. And I think he felt it only right that he lend some kind of support to those who fed the rest of us. Farming is not for those who expect a cheering section.

And the riding was an addiction. There is *nothing* in the world like the smell of an early summer morning in south Georgia. The aromas of pine, new sunshine, and red earth, just turned and still damp from dew, do something to the senses. For a little while it is cool, and you ride with your window down and your elbow out. An all-together proper pose. The same pose struck in the late afternoon. The smells are different, still good: the same red earth, only baked a bit, mingles with the tang of triple-20 and the scent of creek water thrown from giant irrigators. And the ride is slower; an exhalation, with a day of work behind you. More often than not, in my dad's case, there was a Pabst Blue Ribbon clenched between his thighs and several more in a brown paper bag beside him. I don't know why, but I never connected these times with his drinking problem. It was drinking and *riding;* part of the ritual and something, in those days at least, I thought of as entirely innocent.

Saturdays and Sundays were the same, only a bit more structured. Certain roads were taken on Saturday morning, others in the afternoon. Same for Sunday. There were thousands upon thousands of acres of peanuts or soybeans or corn or cotton to discuss or pass judgment on. There were new trucks to look at, new building projects to inspect. After rains, it was mandatory to check the roads for washouts and slick spots. Though my dad didn't hunt, he felt it was his duty to drive the field roads looking for deer tracks and trails. All legitimate reasons to ride.

I wasn't always asked to go on these rides. Sometimes it was weeks between invitations. And even then I didn't always want to go. He would ask and I would decline. Then he would sigh that sigh and I would climb into the truck beside him. It's not that I didn't enjoy the rides, I did. But I was always worried at least one of his buddies wasn't going with us and we would be alone for four or five hours. He rarely spoke when it was just the two of us and the thought of facing the silence did not appeal to me. It was a heavy, uncomfortable silence.

Other times, Sunday mornings especially, I was eager to be asked because the ride meant escape from guaranteed boredom at the voice of the Baptist preacher. And most of the time at least one or two of his buddies were with us, and it seemed another presence made it easier for him to talk to me. I was like the mascot, teased and picked on, and I liked it. In later years, I always managed to sneak a beer or two.

Some of the best times were when I was five or six years old, maybe younger, and we would end up at Mr. Joe's, a small, white wooden building a couple of miles west of town, amongst the pine.

I'm sure there are some in Plains who never acknowledged Mr. Joe's existed. If they did, they probably only whispered about it. A lot of the wives in Plains, I am told, cursed Mr. Joe's place out loud. Mr. Joe's was a place where men went to drink beer and play cards and raise hell. It was always exciting for me to pull up and see any number of pick-up trucks and cars parked haphazardly around the place. Until I reached drinking age, I was allowed only in the front room. The old man would give me a six-ounce Coca-Cola in the bottle and a bag of potato chips and sit me on a stool at the counter and tell me he would be back in a little bit. Then he would disappear into the back room. And I would sit and listen to the men laughing and carrying on and playing cards and wait for somebody to come out and talk to me for a few minutes and maybe buy me another Coke. Every once in a while the front screen door would squeal open and someone I knew of as one of my dad's friends would come in and see me and call me "Little Billy." Then he, too, would vanish into the back room. As far as I recall, I never got bored sitting there. I always felt as though I was part of some secret club; a place little boys weren't allowed to be. This was only enhanced when sometimes, as we were leaving, the old man would say, "Don't tell Mama we were at Mr. Joe's, okay?" And I would nod, very aware of how solemn the situation was. I never told, but Mama always knew.

The riding was something in the blood and a ritual I continued until I moved away. The ride is not the same where I live now. And for the brief period of time my dad was away from Plains, he quit riding, too. It was as if only those old roads could comfort him, could ease his mind. His friends knew this, and up until a few days before he died, one or the other would come by the house and wrap him in blankets and half-carry him to their truck. And he would lean on the door, bundled up like a child, and peer out the window as the old roads went by. Not for hours, as he had when he was healthy, because just the act of walking out the front door would tire him to the point of exhaustion. But for a few minutes, at least, in each of his last days, I would like to think the ride carried him away from the cancer and allowed him to believe, pretend even, all was well on just another summer, Sunday afternoon.

I still ride when I visit Plains, but it is not the same. The roads haven't changed much; the same places become rutted and washboarded after rain. But I have been gone so long now, twenty years, it's as if the roads somehow know I'm a visitor and are reluctant to make my travel easy. And I become almost envious as I see others out riding my roads, posed behind the wheel, as comfortable as I used to be. And it is sad, too, when the others I see are hesitant to throw up their hands in greeting, suspicious, almost, of the unfamiliar man in the unfamiliar vehicle riding down *their* familiar roads.

But then I pass what is now Mama's land and I almost, *almost*, get the feeling I'm back where I belong. The old brick-o-block building, once used for storage, is still there, though it now sits amid a damn-near impenetrable tangle of blackberry, wild plum and pin oaks. It overlooks acreage that, each season, used to be row upon row of peanuts. Most of it is planted in pine now. There was once an old two-room wooden shack on this land that was wired with electricity and was the location for many a card game and the "hat-burning" parties that were held every fall. I don't think anyone really knows how the hat-burnings began, but most people I know credit the old man. In

Plains you created your own entertainment. And the old man could pretty much be counted on to get something started. He was a catalyst of sorts and probably got more people into trouble with their wives and families than anyone would care to admit. One fall night, after harvest, he hosted a poker game and a bonfire at the old shack. Of course, there was much beer and bourbon and a little 'shine consumed. It was in celebration of a good year gone and the beginning of a few weeks of rest before the cycle began again. Most of the men there wore seed caps; stained with sweat and encrusted with a year of red dirt. It is said my father, all aglow with attention and well into a bottle, yanked his off his head and threw it into the bonfire. Dozens more flew through the air after it, beginning a ritual that continued for years. It later became a point of pride for some to wear through the year, then burn, the nastiest hat.

I went to a few hat-burnings, though it was mostly for grown men. But I remember the thrill of being there, of being included. There was the October chill, the light of the fire, and the smell of smoke. I remember seeing farmers who rarely spoke loosen a bit and laugh loud, enjoying a night away from the farm. I remember feeling safe there, in the light, protected from the dark beyond the circle of fire. And there was always a hint of the forbidden, too, with the drinking and cussing and the flicker of flame on all the faces. It was almost tribal. And in the center of it all was my father, laughing and joking and so different from the way he was around home. I remember being proud of him then, and a little awed, that he was the one responsible for such a wonderful thing. But I was also very aware that the next day, at home, he would once again be silent.

Further down from Mama's land are the crossroads. There is a grove of pine where I learned all I was ever going to about hunting from my father. One October, for my twelfth birthday, he gave me a double-barrel, sixteen-gauge shotgun that my mother frowned upon. The day before Thanksgiving he announced we were going deer hunting the next morning. Most of the time, during November in that part of the South, it is cool during the day but not cold. And I have seen several Thanksgiving days where the temperatures reached the low eighties. That particular Thanksgiving, though, when the old man woke me up about 5 A.M., I could hear sleet pecking at the windows. By the time we reached Webster County and the crossroads, we were driving in a full-fledged ice storm. I never thought to question the old man; it just wasn't done. He pulled to the side of the road and led me into the pine grove and found a tree to his liking. I climbed to the lowest branch and he handed me the shotgun. "If you see a deer," he said, "shoot it." I nodded. "And if you get down from this tree, I'm going to whip you. Don't move." I nodded again and he left. I don't remember how long I sat in the tree shivering and listening to the ice-coated pine needles clink and tinkle against each other. It could've been thirty minutes or a day and a half. And as far as I was concerned, the biggest deer in Webster County could've climbed up and sat beside me. I was freezing and I didn't care. I didn't care to the point where I was willing to face the old man's wrath rather than sit in that tree and freeze my little ass off anymore. The sun was rising when I finally climbed down and began to walk. I knew the old shack was a half-mile from the pine grove and I could at least get out of the wind. For some reason it didn't surprise me when I found the lights on and three or four pick-up trucks parked around the place. And I wasn't surprised either when I peeked in the window and saw my old man, along with a few of his buddies, playing poker around the table and drinking Jim Beam from the bottle. To his credit, the old man didn't blink an eye when I sidled in and stood before the gas heater. He never asked me if I saw a deer. He didn't beat my ass, either. My ace in the hole was telling Mama about our "hunting" trip when we got home and he knew it. I kept the secret until he died.

Sometimes I wonder if my father thought I was supposed to come complete, knowing everything a son of his was supposed to know without any instruction on his part. He never had the patience, or felt the need, to explain anything to anybody, much less to one of his own. Questions were often answered with a sigh or a glare or a curt response seemingly designed to make one feel as if they were the most ignorant person in the world. This is a trait of the Carter family and one I am glad is softened by the Spires side of me.

Most of the lessons I learned from my father I learned by watching and listening. And, as harsh as it may sound, I learned at an early age I didn't want to be like him when I grew up. Oh, I admired him and loved him but there was something hard in his personality. Something that scared, to a point, those around him. Even his friends, those who knew him well, were aware of his moods and how quickly they changed. He had no patience, none, and was quick to point out the shortcomings of others. When he quit drinking, ten years before he died, we, my family, looked forward to a new husband and father; a man who could be comfortable with himself and the rest of us. But he didn't change. He just wasn't drunk anymore. If anything, it seemed as if he was just a little more pissed off at the world.

We all know he loved us. This is something I've never doubted. But I often had the feeling he was disappointed in us and felt we didn't quite measure up to whatever his vision of a family was. Little things we did, kid things, infuriated him. And things we had no control over, like childhood illnesses, seemed to confuse and terrify him.

As a child I had asthma. The kind where it seemed there

was a thousand pounds on my chest and I couldn't draw breath for anything in the world. One night, when I was six or seven, I had a particularly violent attack. The things my mother normally did to help me wouldn't work and I had to go to the hospital. I was bundled up in the front seat of our car and my father was driving. I don't remember what happened once we reached Americus, but the trip there is something that will stay with me always. As we sped down 280, at a hundred miles an hour or more, my old man kept reaching over and grabbing my shoulder to shake me. "Breathe, goddammit!" he would yell. "Breathe! Goddammit! Breathe!" His reaction scared me more than the fact there was no air in my lungs. "Goddamn you! Breathe!" We made it to the hospital and he snatched me up and ran in, cursing me and whoever else he saw the whole time. Now, thirty years later, I know he was scared I was going to die. And, in his own way, with his brand of love, he was commanding me not to.

My mother, who was married to him for thirty-three years and knew him best, told me he never truly had a peaceful moment in his life. That he never let his guard down; never accepted for a moment that the world was the way it was going to be, regardless of his opinion. I think she's right. But there were instances when I saw him almost, but not quite, lower his shield for a moment or two and exhale. All those times were when he was doing what he loved best; when he was carrying on where his daddy left off. These times were all at the warehouse, the family business, where he knew he was supposed to be.

Chapter Four

Down on the yard of Carter's Warehouse, our family business, there were several pits in the ground covered with grills of four-inch metal pipes spaced about six inches apart. The pits were located at one end of any number of warehouses and the sheller and the cleaners. Wagon loads of peanuts were pulled across the grills and parked with the front tires snug in a metal sling of sorts and the rear of the wagon at the edge of the pit. The rear gate of the wagon was opened and the peanuts spilled out and down into the pit. When the front of the trailer was lifted by the sling, the remaining peanuts fell in, emptying the wagon. The bottom of the pit was slanted towards an opening and, through gravity, the peanuts fed themselves into metal scoops bolted to a wide belt of canvas that ran in a continuous loop up a narrow, metal elevator. The peanuts were then run through a cleaner that removed clods of dirt, rocks, and the occasional snake or two and then loaded onto another wagon. When the peanuts had been cleaned, the wagon was driven to another pit, dumped again, and distributed, by conveyor belt, into one of three or four huge bins in a huge warehouse. There were several of these elevators and each had metal rungs on its side that led to the very top where the electric motors were. Around the top was a narrow catwalk of grated metal with a railing, thirty feet up; a crow's nest of sorts. This was for maintenance, but, more importantly, it was a place to survey my domain.

Monday through Friday and half a day on Saturday, the yards were filled with people and the clatter of machinery. Trucks came and went, tractors pulled trailers, and dust boiled over everything. There never really was any down time. When it wasn't peanut season, it was cotton. When it wasn't cotton, it was grain. In between, there were pesticides and herbicides and fertilizers to spread. And there was always maintenance going on. But on Saturday afternoons, especially at the end of fall and the first few weeks of spring, the business shut down and the yard emptied. And then I could prowl.

I'd been around the business since I was five years old. The warehouse was within walking distance of school and from my first day of first grade the old man expected me to work. Not that I did much the first few years; I mainly rode around on the back of Frank McGarrah's tractor while he pointed out pieces of trash for me to pick up. And I got in the way a lot. But by the time I was eight or nine years old I was free to roam the yards whenever I wanted. I think it was pretty much a given that one day I was going to run the warehouse; at least *I* thought so. So me being allowed to poke my nose into everything around there was the old man's way of letting me learn. And I wanted to be there, I couldn't help it; it was in my blood.

There was really no set pattern to my exploring; there were so many semidangerous things for me to get involved in. But I always began my time alone on the yards climbing to the crow's nest at the top of one of the elevators. I could see most of Plains from up there and watch Saturday afternoon unfold. And, with the machinery shut down and the people gone, the thousands of sparrows and pigeons that waited patiently for us to leave felt free to feed on the peanuts and grains spilled to the ground. After a half-hour or more some of the feral cats that lived in the sheller crept out to lust after the flock. They never rushed in to grab a bird. I think years of trying and failing by the generations before had been passed down and they knew it was futile, so they sat silently beside the wall, wrapped in their tails, wishing. Sometimes, startled by something I couldn't see or hear, the birds, all at once, would take flight, as if in a panic, to boil about in the air only to settle down a few seconds later to once again feed. Not much as entertainment goes, but something I could watch for hours. And I know, in all the time I sat there dreaming, I had many profound, preteen thoughts; thoughts that could cure all the ills of the world. But for the life of me, there are none I can remember now.

My vigil would end and I would climb down to go explore. Sometimes I would stroll through the cotton warehouse, where all the bales were stored before shipping. The bales were stacked in rows, three or four times head height, and created mazes. It was easy to imagine, as my footsteps bounced from the concrete floor to the metal roof and back again, there were things lurking at the dark ends of those rows. And I would find a place where a bale had been removed, creating a niche, and climb up, cocooned by the kerosene smell of burlap and old dust, and pretend to hide from the things. When the monsters were gone, after I had defeated them, I was free to ramble again. There was usually a visit to the shop, where equipment maintenance and repair was done. And I would ponder big, rusted bolts and old batteries and play with things I wasn't supposed to. Or I would go and gaze in wonder at the purplish-green bruise that stained the ground for four or five feet around the building storing the chemicals. But the best, of course, I always saved for last.

The big warehouses were made of creosote posts and sawmill oak and roofed with tin. The three or four bins in each warehouse were filled with peanuts by a conveyor belt that ran the length of the building at the very top. The peanuts were fed through the pit at one end and carried up to the belt by elevator. There was a wooden walk beside the belt for maintenance and for access to switch the belt from bin to bin. This was all reachable by a wooden stairway at one end of the warehouse. I was always careful to make sure no one was around when I climbed the stairs; I was young, but not stupid.

And I would open the door and peer in at perpetual dusk and listen to the pigeons fly away in surprise. Tiny shafts of light, like laser beams, stabbed through nail holes in the roof and pierced the dust to give me points of reference along the walkway. Above me was a tangle of wooden support beams; below me were oceans, endless depths, of peanuts. Sometimes only six or eight feet beneath me. Other times a dizzying drop of sixteen feet or more would beckon. And I would leap. Time and again, alone, I would leap to land chest deep into the sea, then wade, covered with dust and sneezing, to the ladder on the wall and start all over again. It was my greatest secret and some of my best times. And I would pay to do it again.

The older I got, the more real work I was expected to do. And I took my place beside the men down on the yards; standing in line as bags of fertilizers were passed from hand to hand, from the rear of semis, to be stacked in a storage shed. I pushed brooms for days, it seemed, cleaning the warehouses at the end of the season. And when peanuts were in, the time I wasn't sleeping was spent down on the yards. Everyone worked where they were needed. And there was something to be done seven days a week, twenty-four hours a day. Some farmers had their own trailers to transport peanuts. Those who didn't borrowed trailers from us. And they didn't have time to pick up empties and bring them back full. So there was always someone out driving, sometimes fifteen or twenty miles away, to remote fields to retrieve wagon loads of peanuts. When they were brought in they were weighed on the giant scales beside the office, then put in line to be cleaned or dried. The yard was always a maze of red, metal wagons with tractors and trucks zooming in and out between them. And the red dust was ever-present; invading the pores and lying heavy on the lungs. For a month or more, bath water ran reddish-orange and the skin took its own sweet time returning to its normal cast.

Besides the noise of tractors and trailers and machinery and men, there was the roar of the dryers; a white noise you didn't notice until you listened for it. The wagons had double floors; the top being a metal mesh. There was a rectangular opening at the rear or on the side of each wagon where the metal or wooden mouth of a canvas duct fit snug. The canvas duct was attached to a giant blower that forced heated air, blown over a ring of flame, up through the mesh floor, drying the peanuts. The peanuts were green and damp when they came in from the field and had to be dried before cleaning or shelling.

The dryers ran full time and each wagon load had to be checked every hour on the hour for moisture content. Some of the dryers were housed in a big, corrugated metal building. Others were beneath an open shed with a wooden catwalk running the length of the building over the row of dryers. There was space for sixty or eighty wagon loads of peanuts to be dried at a time. Each wagon was numbered and listed in a book kept in a room at the old sheller. When a load was first brought in, a sample was taken and the moisture percentage was entered in the book. Then the load was backed into a dryer space and hooked up. Every hour thereafter, whoever was in charge of the dryers checked the book and made a list of the loads that needed sampling. The list was split up between two people, each of whom left the sheller with a stack of metal pie pans and an auger. The auger was a six-foot, hollow metal spike, about two-and-a-half inches around, and open along one side and at the top, where there was a handle to hold onto and twist. I'd go to one of the two dryer buildings and walk between the rows, checking my list against the numbers on the trailers. When I found one that matched, I'd sail a pan up into the peanuts, hook the auger to the side, then climb the ladder on the front on the wagon. During the day, I normally didn't hesitate to climb in. At night, though, the overhead lights created deep shadows in the corners of the wagons that, sometimes, hid snakes that had been scooped up in the field and dumped along with the peanuts. The heat forced them to the top. If all was clear, I climbed in and pulled the auger up after me, rammed it into the peanuts, then pulled it out, twisting. The auger was filled with peanuts, and I spilled them out into the pie pan over the number I'd torn from the list I carried. When I was done sampling all the loads on the list, I carried them back to the sheller and the rest of the hour was spent shelling each pan full and putting them into a mysterious black box that told us, through a needle on a gauge, what the moisture content was of that particular load. Then we started all over again. Hour after hour.

My father rarely came home during peanut season except to shower, though the house was only a two-minute drive away. Mama worked there, too, keeping the books, but would leave at meal times to go and cook for us and bring the food to the office. Many nights during peanut season, as a child, I got to stay all night at the warehouse with the old man, sleeping on one of the old sofas in the office. I remember walking down to the dryers with him at the unbelievable hour of 11 P.M. to check on the crew. Sometimes we'd walk down the rows and he'd stop and let me use the tiny thermometer he kept clipped in his shirt pocket to test the temperature of one of the wagons. If it wasn't 120 degrees, I'd hold the flashlight for him while he fiddled with the thermostat. This was all done without words between us, but I didn't care. It was summertime and late at night and I felt the old man was giving me time he didn't normally have. And it never failed, in spite of all my plans to watch the sun rise, that I woke up early the next morning in the office, wondering where the night went. By the time I was twelve, though, the mystery was gone and I worked a full-time night shift at the dryers during the summer months.

I used to wonder why the old man spent so much time at the warehouse. Sometimes it felt as if he loved the place more than he loved us. And I think, in a sense, he did. But it was a love he couldn't help; he was good at what he did; he was born to it. And though he would never have admitted to it, I think he somehow felt he was closer to *his* daddy there, a man he worshipped, who died when my dad was just a boy.

I never knew my Granddaddy Earl. He died in 1953, seven years before I was born. Or I guess I should say I never met him. I knew him from the stories my grandmother told me. And I knew him from the black-and-white framed photograph my old man kept on his dresser. My father was not much for recounting memories; not much for reliving his days as a child. So I somehow knew, even when I was young, the picture, the only one on his dresser, was very special. I remember stealing into my parents' bedroom and peering up at the photo, thinking the strange man behind the glass could see me. It was spooky, because I mistook the tentative smile on his face for amusement at me and I wondered how he knew I was there. Later, when I found out the man was my grandfather, the eeriness faded away to be replaced by a sense of comfort. I felt as though that image of a slightly balding man with wire-framed glasses and a very shy smile somehow gave my dad a bit of peace; kept him as much at ease as he could be, and offered a thread of sorts, a thread allowing him to hang on a bit to what meant most to him. I've often imagined my father, in the gray light of early mornings, standing before the dresser and taking from it the things he'd put there the night before: a pocketknife, his watch, a handful of change, a Zippo lighter, his wallet. And as he put these things in his pockets, I've imagined him looking at the photo of his father and drawing a bit of strength, maybe, or giving silent apology for something he should, or shouldn't, have done the day before.

There is a picture of my grandfather in my house now. Not the formal portrait my old man had. It's more casual: a picture of a man at ease, with his hands in his pockets, standing on the steps of some old house. And he has the same smile; still amused. The eeriness has returned, too, for when I see the picture, a first glance, I see myself. The thread has not been broken.

My father was the youngest, by eight years, of four children. He was the baby and spoiled rotten. By all accounts, my Granddaddy Earl was the biggest offender and allowed my dad to get away with things his sisters and brother would have never dared attempt. They lived on a farm, producing peanuts, cotton, watermelons and syrup, and everybody worked. Later, when my grandfather started the family warehouse business, my dad was expected there every day after school. They worked together, side by side, until July 1953 when my grandfather died. My dad was sixteen years old. If the moment my dad's life went all to hell could be pinpointed, I think this would be it. I've tried to imagine the devastation, but I can't. I do know without my grandfather's hand to guide, my dad began a trip outside the lines that lasted until he died.

The first leg of the trip lasted for ten years. When my grandfather died, my uncle, Jimmy, came home from the Navy to take control of the family business. He was twenty-nine years old and a stranger to my father. My old man, in a very rare moment, told me once that Jimmy was like a character in a book. A character who couldn't be touched; who couldn't be tarnished. I think my grandparents, even, were a bit mystified by their oldest child; a man who shined, a man who had about him the mist of great things to come.

My first thought was that my dad rebelled against my uncle; that he was asserting his right as a teenager to do the things teenagers do. But it was more than that. It was fury. Fury that a man he barely knew could come from far away and take from him something he thought of as his own. My uncle didn't know this; there was a duty for him to fulfill in Plains and that was all he needed. The thoughts and feelings of a teenaged boy, I imagine, were not the things that weighed upon him. And though my grandmother was strong, as strong as any woman I've ever known, the early fifties in south Georgia was not the time for a lady to stand front and foremost in a business given to men. So Jimmy, the oldest of four, gave up his career in the Navy to come back to Plains and take over the warehouse. And my old man was pissed.

Carter family history, since the mid-seventies, has become

a big, gray thing: part fact, part fiction, part PR machine. I ignore most of it and rely mostly on the stories I've been told by those who were there. My grandmother told me once that she had never seen two people as close as my father and grandfather were. From the time he was old enough to walk, my dad was never more than a step or two away from my Granddaddy Earl. They would walk the fields together, she said, while my granddaddy explained to my father how things grew. They later traveled the old roads together, sometimes ending up in Americus at a place my grandfather went to play cards. My old man would wait for him; killing time by getting in everyone's way. Later, he worked at the warehouse with his father, content, I am told, knowing his life was pretty much laid out for him; knowing he was where he was supposed to be.

I know the feeling myself. It's a good one, in most respects, and painful when it's snatched away. So it's not that hard for me to imagine how upset the old man was when he realized his future was not what he'd always thought it would be.

There are not many who would have dared try to get into the old man's head. Some claim to know what he was thinking, how he felt, but I don't think so. I know better. If anyone came close, though, it was my mother, Sybil. She met him when she was ten or so, married him when she was sixteen, and spent the next thirty-three years of his life with him. She is *the* expert on Billy Carter. No one else comes close. So when she tells me the death of Granddaddy Earl was a major disaster in my father's life, I believe her. When she says he went damn near crazy when the reins of the family business slipped from his hands, I believe her. She was there when he began to go wild; she was there when the times were bad and when alcohol became a major part of the old man's life. And she was there, too, to witness the few years of near-peace my old man had when he finally got the chance to take his turn doing what his daddy meant for him to do.

Chapter Five

I've seen a lot of photographs of my dad from when he was young. I'm glad they are there, because without them I don't think I could ever imagine him as anything but a grown man. And it comforts me to know he was once a child; he once could look upon the world and wonder, the way I did.

There is one of him as a baby of three or four, standing in a yard somewhere holding his daddy's hand. Granddaddy Earl is beaming down at him. Another is of him as a tiny thing, held in the arms of the black lady who helped look after him. But the one I can see in my mind as if I hold it in my hand is a high school picture of him taken less than a year after my grandfather died. He has a head full of hair, slick, and combed back in a DA. Other than that one youthful hint, it's as if the grainy black-and-white face is that of a much older man. It's a hard face; the face of someone who is trying his damnedest to look tough and mean. And he's pulling it off. And there are shadows there, too, created by the beginnings of a face he later wore most of the time when there was no one outside of the family to see it. It was the face of one who broods.

By all accounts, my old man led a pretty normal life up until my grandfather died. Afterwards, he was on his own a lot. My grandmother, Miss Lillian, was a teaching nurse and traveled a good bit of the time. Jimmy had the business to run and my aunts, Gloria and Ruth, were married and had families of their own. That's not to say he was ignored by his mother, his brother, and his sisters. He wasn't. It's just that he was cut from the same cloth as the rest of them: headstrong and stubborn. It was very evident to me, in later years, that my grandmother, my aunts, my uncle, and my father all loved each other. But there was a distance between them, as if there was an invisible barrier; a wariness that kept them from truly enjoying each other's company.

The one constant for my father, from the time he was ten or so, was my mother, Sybil. She'd moved to Plains from Clayton, Alabama, with her family in 1948. And my old man was taken with her from the beginning. He used to tell the story of running into my granny, Lucille Spires, at the drug store one day and telling her he wanted to marry her daughter. She took out a piece of paper and wrote a note promising Sybil to him when they were old enough. Five years later they were married. Everyone I know agrees, emphatically, that my mother was the best thing to ever happen to my dad.

My mother says that even then, in those early days, the old man's temper was very evident. She tells of the time they got into an argument about his temper and she broke up with him, giving his ring back. In a rage, he flung it across the road and onto the railroad tracks that ran by my mother's house. And then he left, vowing never to come back. She watched him through her window that night, for hours, as he walked up and down the tracks with a flashlight, looking for the ring. The next day he gave the ring back and nothing was ever mentioned again about the argument. That was the old man's style: never apologize, never explain. And then there's the story of the public fight between my father and my uncle beneath the water tower one Saturday afternoon. I can only imagine most of what went on that day because even those who witnessed it are still, forty-odd years later, strangely reluctant to talk about it. I do know my dad was just a teenager and my uncle was near thirty and not too long out of the Navy. My mother tells me, as far as my father was concerned, that the fight had been building since Jimmy's return after my grandfather died. My dad felt he was quite capable of taking care of his mother and the family business on his own and resented what he thought of as meddling by a stranger, his brother. The actual words or actions that led to blows being thrown are things I'll never know. But one thing is certain; my father and my uncle were no different as far as stubbornness goes, and it is no wonder that blood was drawn when they finally clashed. I asked my uncle about this fight and was surprised by his casual reply. "Oh, yes," he said, "me and your daddy fought several times." Most of the time it was over something that had to do with the business. And my dad would tear out in his truck, slinging red dirt and rock, swearing never to return to work as a "hired hand" for Jimmy. But he would always be back the next day, Jimmy said, an hour or two before anybody else, ready to work, as if nothing had happened. My dad couldn't leave the warehouse. In his heart it was his.

But he did leave for a while. After graduating from high school he joined the Marines. When he got out of boot camp, he and my mother got married. He was eighteen and she was sixteen. In the Marines, my dad learned to drink with the big boys and tried to hone his fighting skills. As far as the skills were concerned, I don't think they took too well. Though my old man was easy to provoke and he never, ever backed down, I don't think he ever won a fight in his life. He told me once that in boot camp they'd convinced him one Marine was the equivalent of seven or eight normal men in strength and other manly things, and he believed them. He said it took several tries testing this and getting his ass whipped before he realized they might have been exaggerating a bit. But he always seemed to glow for a day or two after a fight. I think it was a release of sorts for him.

After he left the Marines he returned to Plains with my mother, two baby girls, a chip on his shoulder, and a drinking problem. In his own words, my father has said he literally hated working for Jimmy; he resented him for taking over the business. And he let it show. He began to drink more, a lot more, and my mother worried about him. She convinced him to try Alcoholics Anonymous, and to her—and his, I imagine—surprise, he did. He chose to attend meetings in Albany, Georgia, forty miles away from the eyes and ears of small-town Plains. Besides, he said, he didn't want anybody around home thinking he couldn't hold his liquor.

For a brief time, three or four months, he quit drinking. But as with most alcoholics, the voice that accompanies you everywhere you go began to tell him he'd been a good boy for long enough; he'd shown them he could quit, and it was okay now to have just a drink or two. So he did, and didn't stop for eighteen years. The voice is persuasive.

I know. The same voice is with me always.

I could write that my father's drinking problems stemmed from the fact he lost *his* father at such an early age and that there was no one there to smooth things over for him. Or that he drank from frustration at things not turning out for him the way he wanted them to. But I don't know this, because not *once* did I ever hear my old man blame his problems on anyone but himself. Not once.

After a couple of years, our family (I was in the picture

now) left Plains with my dad, again, vowing never to return. He tried college for a year at Emory University, then dropped out. We went to Macon, Georgia, where he, miserable, worked in a paint factory for a while. My mother says these were the worst years of her life; living hand-to-mouth in a tiny apartment with four small kids and a husband who drank all the time.

Good times came over the phone in 1962. Jimmy had decided to enter state politics and knew he needed help running the warehouse. Reluctantly, after discussing it with my grandmother, he called my dad and asked if he would come home. If not for that call, I probably would have ended up living in Macon the rest of my life, because the old man would have never returned to Plains unless he was asked. And asked by Jimmy.

My father dealt with the farmers and the hands and Jimmy handled the business end of the warehouse. My Aunt Rosalynn and my mother kept the books and my cousins worked there. And I was only a few years away from my days of becoming a pain in the ass down on the yards. It was the perfect arrangement and a true family business.

Jimmy admits he was surprised at first at how hard my father worked, but I don't think anyone else was. There was no way the old man could have failed at the family business; that would have been like failing his father, something he could not do. And he started beginning his days an hour before sunrise as if the time he spent sleeping was wasted. The warehouse was where his heart was and he nurtured it. He was alive there.

My uncle and my father worked side by side in these years, building the business. In 1966 my uncle made his first run for governor and entered politics full-time. My father ran the business himself and took over full management in 1971, when Jimmy entered the Georgia Governor's Mansion.

If there were happier times for my father, I don't know when they were. He took his responsibilities very seriously. He shined there. There is no way I can count the times I sat in the office watching the old man interact with the farmers. It was a show, to be sure. There were some men who we waited for to come walking through the door. The verbal exchanges between some of these men and my father were fast and furious and wicked and funny. There were stabs and punches and solid knock-outs. And I know for a fact some of those men came by with no business to attend to. They came to try and take on the old man; to spar with him. Others came to watch. But he was a master and very few ever got the best of him. I almost felt sorry for some of those with the national press who came to Plains in the late seventies, with Mayberry on their minds, intending to put the backwoods brother in his place. Almost. The old man was quick, and as sharp as anyone I've ever seen. Even as a child I was amazed. But even in my amazement I wondered why that wit was never shown at home. He somehow switched it off when he walked into the house.

The humor was needed at work because harvest begins about the time a damp blanket of heat is pulled up over the lower extremities of Georgia, and the gnats swarm so thick you can't open your mouth without gulping down a pound or two of unwanted protein. And the work is hard. So the old man joked and played around with most of the farmers and the hands; kept things light while keeping his mind on the business. He treated all the farmers with respect; a respect they'd all earned, the respect they deserved. But there were others he treated differently; some he showed a *great* respect.

There are people in any business who seem to be above all others. It's the same with farming. I know men and women who have given their lives to it; they are what farming is all about. And it is not hard to spot them. They are the ones who walk this world as if they themselves are the land embodied. Quiet people, mostly, who breathe when the earth breathes. People who have in one hand more strength than most of us will ever know. People who can smell rain a day or two away and who know, *know*, the exact moment when a year has gone from good to bad even when the crops stand healthy before them. There are very few of these people left now, but I always knew when one came into the office by the change in my father.

They were mainly the older farmers; men who had done business with my grandfather. And the old man toned down a bit in his dealings with these men, as if in displaying a bit more seriousness around them he was in some way paying homage to his father. And there was a mutual respect between them. Most of the farmers I know want nothing more than to be left alone to do what they do with a minimum amount of interference and to be treated the same way they treat those around them. And my father treated them all fairly, as they knew he would.

Sometimes, a farmer would come into the office and shyly ask for my mother, Sybil, ignoring my dad's attempts to pull them into an argument. Mama did the bookkeeping then and was as familiar with what was going on with some of these men's lives as they were. And they trusted her. They would go into her office, sometimes with a bundle of papers in their hands, and whisper, with an uneasy eye on the door. She told me many years later, after the warehouse was no longer ours, that some of the men couldn't balance a checkbook or read and knew she would help with these things; keeping it to herself. Sometimes my mother talks about how hard it's been being known only as the wife of Billy; that she felt as though she'd never been looked at as a person in her own right. But the farmers knew better; they knew her as Miss Sybil. Mama is like one of those people I mentioned before. She is one above all others.

During those times, in a town like Plains, people depended on each other in a way that couldn't be found in more populated areas. Everyone was connected; tied together by the need to survive. And we *knew* each other. With a knowing that, even now, is hard for me to explain. It's a good feeling, a comfortable feeling; one that I miss. I can write about it and remember it and wish my own sons could experience it. But mostly I mourn that it has faded away. Where it disappeared to, and how, are things I'll never know. But it was good while it lasted.

Even now, I never think of what I did at the warehouse as a job. Working our asses off was just the way we lived, the way things were. And I never once imagined a time I would not be involved in the family business. It was *that* strong for me.

Working is not the only thing I remember from the warehouse. We had some real good times. Times that always seem to be recounted when the family gets together for more than a day or two. Three of my sisters, Kim, Jana and Marle, and I, grew up around the business. We were part of it. The people who worked there tolerated us and we looked at most of them as big brothers and a few as extensions of our father. Kim, Jana and I learned to drive down on the yards. First with tractors, then later graduated to beat-all-to-hell pick-up trucks. Kim's driving in those days is legendary, but something I won't go into because I'm scared of her.

I know now that everything my father had me do was his way of teaching me something. Sometimes, though, his technique left a lot to be desired. I remember one peanut season when I was about nine years old. The elevator at the cleaner had come to a grinding halt, and trailer loads of peanuts were backed up in a line with more pulling in by the minute. My old man was pacing back and forth, furiously puffing on one cigarette after another, and raising hell at whoever was in the area to get the damned thing fixed. The belt had become twisted somehow about halfway up the elevator and would not move. He was told the only way to repair it was to dismantle the shaft, section by section. It would take a full day, at least; something that was unacceptable. But the shaft was narrow; too narrow for a grown man to climb into and maneuver. Then the old man's eyes fell on me.

Without a word, he removed the small panel at the base of the elevator and motioned me over. The other men, I noticed, were looking at him like he was crazy. Daddy gave me a flashlight and said to me words I'd heard a hundred times before: "You don't need to tell your Mama about this." And I climbed through the small hole and up the belt, straight up, using the metal scoops as steps. It was hot and dark and dusty and close. And I was sweating and sneezing . . . and having a ball. When I got near the top, scratched and bleeding, pasted with a mud of red dirt and sweat, and absolutely exhausted, I found the problem to be a simple one. Somehow, one of the buckets had bent and was caught on a bolt. I fixed it. I was a hero. As I began the backwards climb down, I froze. Far beneath me, faint through the metal walls of the elevator, a voice floated up. "Where's Buddy?" I heard my mother ask. When I got down I found my father standing there, staring at the ground. My mother stood before him, with a fist on her hip, furiously stabbing her finger at him. The other men were grinning; witnesses to the rare scene of my old man getting his ass chewed out. He was grinning, too. Work continued, and not a word was said by him to me about the whole thing. But I knew I'd done good.

He had plans for me, my old man, and he was going to make damned sure I was ready when my day came to help run the business. He wanted me to know everything, and as I grew older I was treated more as a hand than a son. Which was fine with me because I was as uncomfortable with the father/son thing as he was. And some of the things I learned from him have stuck with me.

The old man's temper was never far from breaking through. I knew it and everyone else did, too. He often reacted to bad news with a fist through a window or a cursing round that lasted for hours. Or sometimes, in my case, a belt. One night in the middle of peanut season, when I was working the dryers, it began to rain. Hard. The yard was filled with trailer loads of peanuts and this was the worst possible scenario. If they got too wet, they could literally rot in the wagons before we got around to the cleaning and drying process. There were only three of us there that night and we all jumped on tractors and began to pull the wagons into empty warehouses, out of the rain. The dust on the ground quickly turned to thick, red mud. Then the power went out and the only light we had was from the tractors. I was pulling a wagon into a shed where I had already stored five or six others, and when I hit the brakes the tractor locked up and slid through the mud. The front of the tractor rammed into the rear corner of one of the trailers, which didn't give a bit. Instead, it created a deep vee of mangled metal between the headlights of a fairly new, very expensive tractor. And I was mortified and thinking seriously about fading away into the night, never to return. I stayed, though, and finished my shift. That morning, I walked from the dryers to the office knowing I was going to have to go through all kinds of hell before I could go home to sleep. The tractor was parked where everyone could see it and the old man was standing there, fuming. "Who fucked up the tractor?" were his words, if I remember correctly. "I did," I said and told him what happened. Then I stood and waited for my whipping.

He just looked at me for a minute or two, then told me to go home. He never mentioned it again. Mama told me a few days later it was because I told the truth and didn't try to hide it from him. I know I didn't sleep that day; I was too busy floating, amazed at my great, good fortune. As I said, when it came to business, he treated everyone fairly.

I look at those years now as a great adventure. We all do, my sisters and I. And we witnessed the old man in his element, not knowing, then, that good times could not go on forever and ever.

There were a few good years left, though. The old man bought the infamous gas station in 1972. He worked at the warehouse. At the station, he played.

Chapter Six

Before 1975, those who traveled Highway 280 and passed the station saw nothing more than a squat, white building with fly-specked windows fronted by two gas pumps and a lighted Amoco sign. There was no way it could be called friendly looking. And I imagine there were some, down to a damn-near empty tank, who slowed, got a eyeful, heard the faint beginnings of the banjo tune from the movie *Deliverance* welling up around them, then decided to chance the ten miles to Americus, where they could gas up under a well-lit awning and maybe buy a Twinkie or two.

The place wasn't particularly threatening, but it did possess an air of seediness. More often than not, Randy, the black Lab who belonged to Mr. Norman Murray, lay sprawled out in front, barely able to move, waiting for someone to toss him another honey bun. There was always a litter of cigarette butts and beer tabs and peanut shells at the foot of the old wooden seats against the front wall of the building. The seats, years before, had been rescued from the Plains High School auditorium during a period of renovation. Four or five wooden Coke crates were there, too. Perfect for propping feet or sitting on when the seats were full. The seats were backed by a big mullioned window that was obscured by stickers and posters and beer signs. Above the window was a big, square RC Cola clock that hadn't worked for years. There was a Lance cracker machine and Coke machine outside for those who didn't want to brave the interior. A metal awning attached to the roof covered a concrete pad that ran from the front door to the pump island. The concrete was stained with years and years of oil, and a black, rubber hose snaked across the pad. It was attached to a bell that clanged obnoxiously every time a car rolled over the hose.

To the left of the main building was a small, tin shack where we kept all the tools. In front of the shack was the rack, or lift, that was operated by an air compressor and was so old we'd prop it up with metal pipes. It was either that or risk an LTD crashing down on our heads in the middle of an oil change. The concrete floor of the shack was two inches thick with decades of grease and dirt, and if a metal tool was dropped, it hit with a muted thud.

In between the two buildings was an open aisle of sorts, about twelve feet wide. There was a rack of tires there and the back part, where the tire changing machine was, was roofed. The machine, an amazing contraption by Plains standards, reminds me of its existence every day by the scars on my knuckles. There were always at least two grills in that open area, made from fifty-five-gallon drums cut lengthwise, in half, and hinged. The insides of the grills were pretty crusty. We counted on the next fire to sterilize and burn away the remnants of the last cookout.

Behind the station was a big pecan tree where we parked. Beneath the tree was a big, wooden, wire spool, where we sometimes sat and drank beer. There was an open oil ditch that ran from the back of the tool shack to the vacant lot behind it. This was before the E.P.A. came to Plains.

Inside, the station was part convenience store and part clubhouse. And there was definitely an air of honky-tonk about the place. The floor was worn tile with big patches of bare concrete showing through in places. To the left, through the door, was a wall covered with calendars and posters and advertisements. Phone numbers and names and semi-crude messages were scribbled on the bare Sheetrock. A big, plastic steer's head, from God knows where, was mounted above it all.

To the right was the bar—a big, wooden L-shaped thing with a Formica top. A small section of the short end of the L flipped up on hinges. Beneath the bar there were three big coolers. One, a red Coca-Cola chest with embossed, white letters on front. All were filled with the coldest beer in Sumter County. Behind the bar was a wall of shelves stocked with all the necessities: blue cans of potted meat and Vienna sausage, flat cans of sardines, dime packs of crackers, cards of pocket combs and radiator stop-leak, potato chips and cheap oil. Everything.

The cash register was behind the bar and so was the phone. When it rang, whoever was closest picked it up and said, "Station." That's all that was needed. Sometimes, it was one of the older widowed ladies in town needing her car jumped off. This was not unusual; some of these ladies drove cars twenty years old or more and terrified us all on the rare occasions when they took them out. If the phone rang after five in the afternoon, very often frantic gestures at the bar indicated who was not there; the men became invisible. I've personally lied to many of the wives in town at one time or another.

My old man bought the station in 1972 from Mr. Mill Jennings. I don't how long Mr. Mill had the place, but he and the station were fixtures in town and had been for years. Before my dad bought it, the only occasions I had to go there were on Halloween, when Mr. Mill stood out front and dropped candy into our bags, or when I walked down the street from Grandma's house to buy a cold drink. I knew it was a place where men hung out; gathered around in front, watching the town go by. And it was rumored there was an old soft drink machine inside that dispensed beer if only you knew the right combination of coins.

I remember being pretty much surprised when I found out the old man was taking the station over. A lot of people were, I think. Years later he told me he'd always wanted to own his own beer joint. The fact that the town council had only recently voted to allow beer sales within the city limits only cemented his decision. Sunday trips to the bootlegger for him and his friends became a thing of the past. They had a key now.

And I think the old man was honored in a way. Mr. Mill told my dad he was the only one he could count on to run the place the way it should be run. It was high praise and a great compliment, and I know for a fact that the old man did Mr. Mill proud. Mr. Mill claimed to have retired but he came by every day just the same. It wasn't long after that he became sick, then died.

Mr. Mill had always been known as a fine man, but it wasn't until we began to clean the station out and move his things that I discovered how good he was. The place was piled high inside with car parts and equipment and all the things needed to run a business. And Mr. Mill never threw anything away. There were paths to the cash register and the restroom and the drink boxes. Against one wall was a massive steel safe under an avalanche of paperwork. In that pile of paper we found several checks, some fifteen or twenty years old, that had never been cashed. There were bundles of tickets, totaling thousands of dollars, that had never been sent out for payment. Some were made out to people I knew could not have afforded to pay. And Mr. Mill had known, too.

Though I had never spent that much time in the station before 1972, it's hard to imagine the atmosphere changing much when the old man took over. The same people I'd seen hanging around all those years were still there. The old man had the place painted and he put in a bar. He got a beer license then hung some plastic, lighted beer signs in the window. And then downtown Plains had its very own honky-tonk.

It was a scandalous thing. Even though everyone in town knew a nip or two was taken at the station on a daily basis, and no one was really bothered by it, it seems that making it legitimate somehow made it more sinful. But if there was anyone in Plains, Georgia, who didn't give a damn about what other people thought of him, it was my old man. He'd finally found a place that was his, and his alone. And, by God, he was going to run that place the way he wanted to.

The station could have been anywhere, I suppose—any building, any lot. Or maybe nothing more than an open space surrounded by trees in a forest somewhere. The place didn't really matter . . . the station was more attitude than location anyway. I'm sure the walls of the physical building, that squat, white ramshackle pile of wood, were soaked with the residue of the past, when Mr. Mill owned the place. More ghosts. But then again, it was all attitude back then, too. No, the station was more a place in time than anything else. And there are some, I guess, who would think I make more of that time than there really was. But that's okay. They weren't there. For me it was a time when all the right people, all the right bits and pieces of what makes a damn-near magical place magical, came together.

Plains was still thriving then, on its own, without the

tourists and the press. The town wasn't a backdrop. It was a real place with real people. None of us were actors then, or extras. It was the time *right* before discount stores and microwave ovens or cable TV. We were all still dusty and sweaty and country as hell. We were comfortable with where and who we were and didn't know we were soon to be considered cute and quaint, almost backwards, in the eyes of those from bigger places. And we wouldn't have cared even if we had known.

Each and every person who came through the doors of the station added something to the place; made it what it was. The locals, though, gave it life. Mr. Norman Murray. Malcolm Wishard. Mr. Robert Paul. Leon Johnson. Mr. George Whitten. Randy Coleman. Dewey Paradise. Mr. Jack Pugh. Bud Duvall. God, there were so many; too many to list. I wish I could. But they all knew they were part of a time that was special. Not then, maybe. Then, it was just the way things were. But later, after it was over, they all might've felt something missing. And I'm sure there are some, like me, who still long a bit for those days.

They were all characters, to be sure, and each one of them had amazing stories to tell. But the greatest character of all, the one from whom the station got its soul, was the old man. Atop the awning, in red, plastic letters about a foot high, was the legend JENNINGS SERVICE STATION, left there in homage to Mr. Mill. Even so, there was no doubt the place was Billy Carter's.

On weekdays we pumped gas, changed oil, fixed tires and sold beer. The regulars came and sat for a while, dispensing wisdom and making observations. The front of the station was always a clutter of pickup trucks. Inside, a perpetual game of gin rummy was going on with one or two half-stoned locals coaching the players with unwanted advice from over a shoulder. We could count on a few, those who had permanent positions in the seats out front, to give running commentaries on how many times Mr. So-and-so passed by on 280 and speculation on where he may be going. Gossip ran rampant, but no less than that spouted by those across 280, on Main Street. The difference was those of us who frequented the station sinned openly. The others, those who whispered and tsked, sinned only when they *thought* no one else was around. They bought their beer in Americus, nine miles away, and made it to church on time every Sunday morning. But the kudzu telegraph hummed mightily and more often than not we knew how much alcohol was in the trunks of their cars, and where they bought it, before they made it back to the blinking yellow light in Plains. In a town of 750, we counted on each other for entertainment.

After 5 P.M., and every Saturday, the station was transformed. And the transformation came when the old man entered. He was a small storm in an enclosed area. Long, hot and humid summer days somehow livened a bit when he came through the door, as if he brought with him the power to recharge the place. He was profane and funny and loud. He was the master storyteller; he was the clown. He was the king.

Even though it was hard not to compare the way he was at the station, around his friends, with the way he was at home, I still basked in the glory of being his son. He was amazing. Conversations stopped when he spoke and heads turned his way. Mundane happenings became events when he told of them. There are some people in this world who seem to be perpetually pissed off, around whom most of us are naturally wary. But the old man pulled no punches with these guys and kidded and teased them as mercilessly as he did the rest. And they didn't seem to mind. He knew everybody and could talk on any subject. And, my God, he could drink.

I think if there is one thing that really upsets me about the impression the press left with most people about my dad is that he reeled around town every day half-drunk. This is not true. As far as I know, the old man *never* drank at work, and most of the people he did business with would attest to that. If he did, he kept it very well hidden. And that would have been as far out of character for him as anything I could imagine, because he was not shy at all about his drinking. But business was business and it wasn't until a few years later, when he'd left the warehouse, that he began drinking full-time.

He drank after work and on weekends. And most evenings, he was home after only a few beers at the station. Oh, there were times when I'd hear his truck pull into the yard hours after all the lights were out and everyone else had gone to bed. Plenty of 'em. But I can honestly say, from my point of view, he never let his drinking interfere with his running the warehouse. Besides, he once told me, it was a point of pride not to admit to a hangover.

And the station was different. It was another place I never connected with my dad's drinking problem. Hell, if you were there, you drank. It was a place where hard-working men wound down after a day or week of *hard* work. Farmers and truck drivers and factory men. And even though the crowd and the atmosphere were right for potentially bad things to happen, I don't recall more than two or three incidences of violence ever occurring. Most of the men who entered the place after five knew they were instant targets. Some, I suppose, would have been disappointed if no one tried to get a rise out of them. And it was comical to see how quickly manners surfaced from these dusty, sun-baked men if one of the local ladies came by for something. Language suddenly became clean and shy "ma'ams" floated around the place. Sometimes a beer was pushed away or hidden discreetly behind a back when some grown man's third-grade teacher pulled up for gas.

The station was definitely a social place. Most mornings there were one or two local retired guys waiting for the door to open at 7 A.M. After the pumps were turned on and the floor and bar were cleaned up from the night before, somebody was usually sent across the street for coffee. And while the coolers were filled from the stock in the back room, events of the previous day were discussed or comments were made about items in the local paper. All the while, gas was pumped for the early risers—farmers, mostly. By mid-morning there was a rhythm. Truck and tractor tires to fix, oil to change, basic mechanic work to do. Lunch was either barbecue from Mr. Joe's or a plate dinner from across the street. And there was constant carrying-on by the people who came and went, and came again, throughout the day. Some, those who'd been up since before first light, started drinking beer about two or three in the afternoon. And then the magical hour of five arrived and the station became an honest-to-God beer joint that just happened to sell a little gas on the side.

For four or five hours there were all kinds of hell being raised. Drinking and gambling and cussing. On Friday and Saturday nights the grills were lit and we ate steaks or chicken or whatever happened to be in season. Mr. Norman Murray, the undisputed fishing champion of the crowd, would sometimes crank up his deep fryers and cook catfish or mullet or bream. He'd make piles of fried potatoes and hush puppies. Everybody contributed. And even if they didn't, everybody ate. You could just walk up and grab a plate. The wives came to eat and sometimes the children. Word spread among the town dogs, Jake and Randy and Pal, and they waited on the fringe for scraps to be thrown their way. We'd sit, with paper plates on our laps, out front on soft drink crates or the wooden seats or on the low concrete walls around the rack. And the old man would beam. It was *his* place. He was with *his* people. And we had fine, fine times.

After the food was gone, and the wives and the children, serious drinking began and the dice came out. Wads of hard-earned money were piled upon the cooler only to be swept away time and again by whoever was hot that night. Entire paychecks were sometimes lost. Minor arguments broke out. And the beer flowed. Out back, beneath the big pecan tree, the more adventurous could always find a pint or two of store-bought liquor or maybe a quart of 'shine under a truck seat. And by ten o'clock, eleven at the latest, the crowd was gone and the lights were out.

I was only twelve years old when the old man bought the station, so I wasn't around the first few years for the night-time events. Mama demanded I be home by dark. But I con-sidered myself to be one of the crowd. I worked there on weekends and during the summer when it wasn't peanut sea-son. There are some who would probably say I got in the way a lot; they're probably right. But I did my part, too. And I learned how to shoot craps there. I won eighty dollars one Saturday afternoon when I was twelve and took it across the street to the Mercantile and bought a bicycle. I was very proud until Mama asked me where I got the money. When she found out, she made me take the bike back and return my winnings. The men at the station refused to take it, though, and taught me how to keep my mouth shut. I learned how to lie. In later years, I became an expert at sneaking beers and worked many days at the station accompanied by the hum of a constant buzz. I loved the place. And when the old man was there, I loved it more.

My old man was one of those people who took over a room when he walked through the door. It didn't matter what kind of mood he was in. If he was happy, it was good times for all. If he was pissed off, everybody got a piece of it. Either way, I watched him with a fascination I still wonder about today. I couldn't help it. Without knowing he was doing it, I think, he demanded attention. And it amazes me still that he received that attention, and a certain loyalty, from so many people. And still does, ten years after his death. He wasn't physically imposing at all; he was short and stocky and wore clunky, black, horn-rimmed glasses. He stuttered when he was excited and had a nervous laugh that signaled one of two things to those who knew him well: either he was genuinely amused or he was on the brink of a serious show of temper. For those of us who were close to him, as close as one could get to my father, the one indication it was time to leave and leave fast was when he looked at you over the top of his glasses and the life, somehow, seemed to have been sucked from his eyes. The pupils shrunk to damn-near invisible points, and you could almost feel a wave of cold coming off his face. Those who have had that look laid upon them have never forgotten it. It was a scary, scary feeling.

But, in spite of his moodiness, and it was legendary, I still admired how he could hold a crowd in his hand. No one was safe from his sarcasm and his wit. Some actively sought it. And, my God, I was amazed at the number of people he *knew* and counted as his friends. He seemed to know everybody and could ask about their families by name. People I never knew existed come up to me on my trips home and tell me how much they miss the old man and give me stories about how he helped them, or someone they knew, out of trouble or with a problem. The old man was free with money and favors and a friend was a friend for life. Or so he thought. But Plains was on its way to changing.

And that's why the four all-too-brief years from when he bought the station until the spring of 1975 mean so much to me. That little bubble of time seemed as if it would hold forever. That time meant the same to my father as it did to me. It is when I like to think of him as being at his best. He'd been running the family business for a while and had proven to himself and everyone else involved—the rest of the family, mainly—that he did it better than anybody. The account books didn't lie. And I think he was almost content for a while; content with knowing that if somehow *his* daddy came back, he could show him all was well and that those walks through the fields had not been wasted.

And he had the station. *His* place. A place that got its life from him and reflected the way he looked at the world. Yeah, it was a dirty, little place, and at any given time you could walk in and find a drunk or two sitting around bitching about farm prices or wondering if the goddamn Braves were ever going to make the playoffs. But that was okay, because if you were there, you somehow automatically belonged. We laughed a lot there. A whole lot. And nobody ever went hungry if they could only wait around a while. If money was tight and you needed a tank of gas and a six-pack or two to take you to Friday, that was no problem. The old man would hold the ticket for a while or not deposit your check until you asked him to. And there was always a dog hanging around somewhere; an absolutely positive sign that there was at least one good thing to be said about the people who frequented the place.

I don't really know if the old man ever made any money from the station and I don't think he cared. What mattered was that he had a place to go. A place he was accepted as Billy Carter before he became "Billy Carter."

And, yeah, the beer was cold.

Chapter Seven

When I look back on the times that I was growing up, I often remember myself as being on the fringe of things, watching and listening. None of us, my mother, my sisters and me, ever seemed to be the center of attention. The old man was the core, the catalyst, of our family. Nothing much ever happened without his approval. And we always seemed to be waiting for him—to come home, to speak, to go to bed, to go away. It's almost as if we were accoutrements to his vision of family life. But that was okay, for me. I was content most of the time to stay out of the way and had a lot of places to hide whenever I felt the need. And my sisters all had their ways of dealing with the old man's lack of attention. Mostly we bumbled through the first fifteen or sixteen years of our lives the way every child does—completely clueless.

My mother, though, was in a constant state of disquiet. It was not easy being Billy Carter's wife. She was the buffer between him and the rest of the world. For the world's sake as well as his own. A million excuses for him passed her lips. A million apologies were made. And she readily admits that for years she was his enabler. Some alcoholics seem to possess great and mysterious powers. Powers that allow them, over a period of time, to pull those closest to them into the hole they've dug for themselves.

I wonder sometimes how hard it was for my mother to smile when that was the last thing she wanted to do. I wonder how many times she assured my sisters and me everything was all right when it really wasn't. And I wonder how many times she held her head up and walked through a crowd as others whispered when she passed. A lot, I bet. She had no choice. Those strange and mysterious powers my father had over her and the rest of us would allow no different.

To some, I suppose, it is unimaginable that one person could have such control. And I have seen the looks in the eyes of those who have not experienced life with an alcoholic family member when I try to explain what it was like. There is a flicker behind those eyes sometimes that conveys a mild disgust that someone could be so weak of will as to allow alcohol to take over their lives. And many times I have sensed the unspoken question as to why we put up with it. It's very simple, really: we loved him. Just as we would have loved him if he'd had the misfortune to be stricken with any other horrible disease. But alcoholism does not begin as a physical affliction; there are no outward signs to warn others away. It is something that begins in a person's soul, growing slowly, to eventually wrap them, and the one's closest to them, in a foggy, fucked-up hug.

I would never pretend to think I could get into my father's head and know what was going on in there. Some have tried and it is laughable. I do know his alcoholism took over damn-near most of his waking hours. When he wasn't drinking, he was thinking about when and where his next drink was coming from. This is something he admitted to. The number-one thing with an alcoholic is to feed the habit; that's all that matters. But even with that horrible thing pecking at his brain, he had a form of self-discipline that was amazing. As I've said before, he never drank at work. And, until the year before he was mentally and physically consumed by the disease, he never drank at home. A minor feat, I suppose, to those who don't understand, but impressive as hell to those of us who do.

Now would be the place, I guess, to write about the times we were embarrassed or hurt by the things he did. The times before the press came along and he went public and the whole country knew he had a problem. But I won't. Those times belong to my family and me. They are ours. They are his. And it is enough for me to know that, in spite of those times, he loved us. More than enough.

It is tough growing up in the shadow of someone. Tougher still when it is the shadow of someone you love. And it would be easy to excuse my old man for his drinking and the problems it caused by saying he was overwhelmed by whatever imagined pressures he faced in trying to live up to an ideal set down by his family. But he knew what he was doing and he never made excuses. He never apologized. And I won't do it for him.

Some would say he became lost when his father died; that he had no guidance through his teens. His buddies tell me this is the time he began to show his ass, to butt heads with anybody with a hint of authority. This is not surprising. Most of the Carters I know are not shy at all about voicing their opinions, and they sure as hell aren't afraid of attention. But there was always someone for my father to turn to. Even though his brother and sisters were much older and had established families of their own, they were there for him. And my mother, since they'd met, had been a constant, calming figure in his life. So he was not alone.

And, of course, there was Grandma—Miss Lillian. If anyone at all could lay a hand upon my father's shoulder and
speak reason he would listen to, it was she. Most of those
long, silent Sunday rides the old man and I took together
ended up at her house in town or the Pond House, where she
lived the last few years of her life. The house was set back off
a dirt road, about two miles from town, hidden by a grove of
pine and dogwood and azalea. It was actually the second one
built on that piece of land. The first had burned down years
before. When my grandmother joined the Peace Corps and
went away to India for two years, my father and my aunts and
uncle decided to rebuild it for her.

There was a big, floor-to-ceiling picture window beside the
front door and the whole living room was visible from outside.
During baseball season she sat in front of that window, in a
hideous, orange-colored easy chair, watching the games on TV.
There was never any doubt she could see she had company, but
sometimes, depending on who was visiting, she would ignore
the knocks on the door or the rapping on the window.
Grandma did not like to be disturbed when the Braves played.
I never saw her deny entry to my dad, though. More often than
not, if there *was* a game on, these visits passed silently but for
occasional curses from either my grandmother or my old man
at a play or a call they didn't like. I knew better than to inter-
rupt and grew to love baseball as much as they did from those
visits. Grandma had one of the first satellite dishes I'd ever seen
installed at the Pond House just so she could watch ball games.
And professional wrestling. I remember, as a child, riding the
fifty miles or so to the Municipal Auditorium in Columbus
with her every few weeks. It was an amazing thing for me to see
my grandmother scream for blood down by the ropes as her
hero, Big Bill Brumo, slammed the bad guys around. It made
me proud.

Grandma taught me how to play poker, a game both she and my old man took very seriously, and she let me smoke cigarettes out at the Pond House when no one else was around. I think she was the first person I'd ever known who was actually content with the way they were living their life. She did what she wanted to do and said what she wanted to say. And it was obvious all four of her children admired these traits and took them as their own.

I always thought of Grandma as some kind of royal entity, and I guess she was; she was the queen of the family. The few family gatherings we had each year revolved around her. Christmas mornings were spent at her house for breakfast. I should say *early* morning, because if you arrived at 5 A.M. you were late. We had good times at these events, but there was always, just beneath the surface, a contest of sorts between the personalities there. Nothing visible, of course, because this was something etiquette would not allow, but between my grandmother and her children their gathered personalities were damn-near strong enough to feel. It was almost as if I squinted my eyes a bit I could see their spirits flowing from their bodies, in bright, vivid colors, to grapple with each other above all of our heads. They were that strong. And each one of them was capable at any time to piss off the entire room with just a word. And they knew it.

But Grandma kept everyone in check most of the time, and they all deferred to her in most matters. Or at least pretended to. And though I'm sure there are those who would argue this, I think my father felt he was closer to her than any of the rest of his siblings. Some would say it was because he was the baby of the family and was treated as such but, whatever the reason, I think their relationship gave him a sense of peace to a point. And it is a testimony to how much his drinking affected him in later years that it became obvious he no longer paid any attention to what she said to him. He would not have done anything to hurt her or embarrass her if not for alcohol.

Sometimes I wonder how it would have been to belong to a family that followed the natural rhythm of families. I wonder if all of us would have evolved differently. Would our tragedies have been greater or less than they have been? I wonder if the successes we've all had would have become major ones in a family of "normal" people? Would we all have lived forever and ever?

It's pointless to wonder, I know, but sometimes still I like to think about how things could have been. There is some comfort there. But there is comfort, too, in knowing that most of us somehow survived the weird and strange times we went through and that they are finally over.

Because when those weird and strange times came, they came with damn-near no warning. And when they were gone, the time of "the way things used to be" had vanished.

Chapter Eight

When I think back on the first fifteen or sixteen years of my life, it is hard for me not to cringe a bit at the image I presented to the rest of the world—that of a goofy-assed kid. But I couldn't help it; that's what I was. And then I catch myself longing a bit for those days and decide maybe it wasn't so bad being exactly who I was, goofiness and all.

The best parts of those times, though, are now, when I tell stories to my sons about where they come from. I see a longing in their eyes for things they never knew. My times roaming the woods and wandering the dirt roads become the great adventures I never realized they were. The bottle graveyard, the buried boxes of treasures, the bike rides to Granny's house, Plains on a Halloween night, and Mason jars full of lightning bugs become magic things they wonder why I ever gave up and left behind. They seem to feel and smell and taste the same things I did as if somehow they experienced these things themselves. And then I realize they are Southern boys and half their blood runs with bits of deep red Georgia clay. Then I tell the story of how my mama and her sister, Lila Ruth, when they were little girls, would have their feet tallowed to help keep them warm at night in a cold Alabama farmhouse. Or how they made mud pies adorned with chinaberries to sell to my great-granddaddy for nickels and then wait on the fence for the rolling store to come by. Story after story I tell them, about the farmers and the sawmill men and the soldiers and the nurses and the thieves and the mule traders. I tell them about their great-great granddaddy getting shot in the back and dying on the ground as his son witnessed it all. They hear of the good things their people did and the bad things. They hear about the preachers and the politicians and about how their great-granny was considered by many to be the kindest lady in the county and who could flat cook the hell out of a blackberry cobbler.

And sometimes it is with a start I realize these stories are not my own. They belong to those who came before me and have somehow melded with my memories as if I have lived them myself. I hope one day to hear my sons tell these stories as if they are as familiar with them as I am. They will have other stories, too, much different from mine. Their Southern blood mingles with that of their ancestors who fled Russia on foot to make their way to America and that of their great-grandmother who told of waking one morning as a child to see Indians peeking through the window of her log cabin in the wilds of Canada. Their blood is strong.

So, as I think back on it now, it should not have been that unusual for someone in our family to aspire to be president. It was somehow in the blood. And, as for every other person in this country, the way was laid out and smoothed over years and years before by all those great-great granddaddies and great-great grannies. The opportunity is there for anyone.

In the mid-1970s, Plains was still in that gee-whiz, Mayberry-like stage of its existence. We'd had a taste of the outside when Jimmy became governor, but not a whole lot. Besides, all that governing went on in *Atlanta*, for God's sake, a world and a half away. And I sure didn't know my uncle was making plans for bigger things. As far as I knew he was planning on leaving the Governor's mansion and coming back home to work in the family business. I don't remember the family's reaction when he first told of his plans. The story goes that when he told my grandmother he was going to run for president, she asked, "President of what?" But it wasn't as if a bomb had been dropped or anything like that. I wish it had been, though. Maybe then we would have had warning of all the hell to break loose in the years that followed.

But as it was, for a while at least, things went on pretty much as they had been. There'd been no formal announcements made. I didn't think of it as real. Peanuts still needed to be processed and there was gas to be pumped. I was fifteen and gave less than a damn about politics.

I heard things, though. Things that amazed me with their meanness. More so when some of the things I heard came from the mouths of people I'd known all my life; people who I considered to be my friends. It had never occurred to me to look beneath the surface of the everyday life I was living, to look behind the smiles. There'd been no reasons to. But then I began to hear the hateful laughter and the jokes and the snide comments. I learned that things weren't always what I thought they were, what I wanted them to be. Only the beginning of lessons I've continued to learn.

My family has a history of doing things that tend to piss off a lot of people. Things like insisting blacks deserve as much of an education as whites; that they had as much of a right to be treated fairly in trade as anyone else; that they should be left alone to live the way they wanted to. It's a fine history; one I am proud of. But these causes were definitely

not popular in south Georgia years and years before and during the time I was growing up. Still aren't in more parts of my
home state than I like to admit.

But my people are hard headed and outside opinions were
nothing more than minor aggravations. My Granny never
allowed the whispering to keep her from filling cardboard
boxes with food taken from the shelves of the grocery
store/gas station she and Granddaddy operated and giving
them away. Grandma never worried a bit when she drove the
dirt roads, with her nurse's bag beside her, visiting those not
welcomed at the county hospital. And the morning the office
door of the family business was found piled with garbage and
the words "nigger lover" scrawled across the brick wall, the
trash was quietly cleaned up and the words were washed away.
The decision to trade with a communal farm in the area had
not set well with some of the locals.

But while most of the family did the things they did in a
quiet manner, Jimmy was different. He had in his heart to
force people to look openly at the way things were. And there
were some who hated him for it. Still do, I imagine. So when
word began to trickle out he was planning a run for the presidency, the information was met with outright hostility from
some in the area. The bad blood was years old, dating from
the time Jimmy started in local politics; a game as brutal as the
one the big boys play. And there seemed to be a peculiar
resentment amongst others that one of their own would dare
try and do good for himself. There was a bewildering shift, a
realignment, of attitudes in the town. People I'd known all my
life suddenly seemed reluctant to speak. Men who were fixtures at the station, who could be counted on to come by daily
for an hour or two, stopped their visits, never to come through
the door again.

But I was fifteen and not yet aware of how strongly people

felt about certain issues. I knew we were Democrats and never thought there might be some Republicans around. Didn't really care. I also knew there was a constant interest in what the government was doing about farm prices and such, but considered myself lucky it was something I wouldn't have to be concerned with for at least a few more years. Then there were the racial issues. And I can't even pretend I didn't know what was going on there. Hell, I lived in the Deep South. I am fortunate not to have been witness to the times of violence; those times had passed. But the attitudes remained. Most of the time there was an attempt at masking these attitudes with a hideous gentility that exists, in some forms, to this day. At other times, depending on the surroundings or the company you were in, the attitudes were much more open, much more honest, and floated about like an invisible filth you could almost feel on your skin. But you ignored the epithets and the crudeness and went about your day the way you always had. At least I did.

Jimmy didn't, though, and never had. As far as I know, he'd never had a fear of speaking out on what he believed in; he never backed away from those beliefs. It's the way he lives his life. But there were those who didn't like it and felt he should keep his opinions to himself and said as much. And in a small town it is hard to hide divisions. I suppose there had always been a rift of sorts between those who believed in what Jimmy stood for and those who didn't, but it was a rift that could easily be ignored as long as it stayed in its place, stayed in Plains. In every town in the country there are those who the other citizens think are trying to get above their raising. And that's okay, as long as they only try; as long as they stay where they're supposed to. But Jimmy went national and the rift in town got wider and deeper.

The changes were not immediate, but when they started it

was as if twenty or thirty years in the life of the town were somehow compressed into only four. The normal ebbs and flows, the rhythms, were disrupted. Just a trickle began it all, to be followed by a huge wave of strange times that receded, five years later, to leave Plains, and some of the people who lived there, in an odd state of post-fame shock.

Some would consider what happened to Plains to be a stroke of great fortune. And I suppose they're right in some respects. There was a lot of money made. And for a few years there was a great show staged that you could sit back and watch for free; the tourists were a constant source of entertainment. The world came to us, bringing with it things some of us would have never had the opportunity to see.

But the experience was not entirely a good one. And I wish now I'd had the foresight to sit quietly by on the sidelines to take note, from beginning to end, of the changes that took over our town. The notes would tell the story of an amazing transformation. A transformation of my family and me. A transformation of the town and of the people who called it home. And a transformation of my old man.

But in the beginning I was as caught up in the weirdness as anyone else. We were all blindsided. And by the time the chance came to clear our heads, it was too late. The wave had come and it was a struggle just to catch our breath.

Chapter
Nine

Plains is no different from most other towns of its size. It is very small, to be sure, but it has a strength, a solidity, that reflects the character of those who built it. People who work hard and depend on the elements for survival; people whose beliefs and ethics and faith have remained the same for generations. It's a very straightforward way of life. And the fact that the population has pretty much stayed the same, around 750 or so, says to me the people like the way they live and don't much give a damn about what others may think.

So in 1975, when the first "outsiders" began to ease into town to check the place out, we were all more than a little amused and entertained. It was obvious what some of the press thought of our town; you could see it on their faces. The first to arrive came with an attitude that they had somehow been exiled to the faraway fringes of the political scene. At the time, Jimmy was nothing more than a humorous story about a one-term Georgia governor who dared to think he might have a chance at becoming president. It was a cute story, and became cuter when Plains was thrown into the picture.

The people from the newspapers and the magazines were easily identified. They wore the expressions on their faces and the Nikons around their necks as if they were badges or armor. They walked the streets like explorers from other planets sent to investigate some new and unusual culture. Some carried about them an air of superiority guaranteed to piss the locals off. Others, the ones from large, metropolitan areas, spoke to the residents slowly and distinctly, as if trying to communicate with feeble-minded children.

A thousand pictures of the town dog sleeping in the street were taken and a man in overalls was worth a roll of film or two. Main Street could be covered in its entirety with one frame, so it became a favorite subject. And our blinking, yellow traffic light—the only one in town—was written about time and again.

But their obsession with peanuts was the funniest thing of all. It was as if these reporters and photographers themselves had discovered the things. I can't count how many times I was asked directions to an honest-to-god peanut field. The question always brought a few laughs because Plains was surrounded by them. From the middle of town a fifteen-minute walk in any direction landed you ankle deep in plowed and planted ground. The directions were always given with a warning, though, to be careful about roaming around uninvited on someone's land. As in any rural area, the town folk and farmers were a bit wary of people they didn't know. But, soon, camera crews became a common sight and it was not unusual to see them stalking farmers on tractors through the fields while choking on a cloud of red dust.

And then Jimmy's bid for the presidency became more than just a human interest story, and the town became crowded with people from the press. They were a constant source of entertainment with their laminated press badges and their aluminum cases and their questions. A few of the first actually came into the station and tried to appear inconspicuous; tried to blend in with the local boys. They failed miserably. To be fair, I know I would have been as out of place in New York or Washington or Chicago as they were in Plains. The culture shock itself must have been tremendous. And in the beginning we were as wary of them as they were of us.

In those days, there were four very distinct types of news people. The first were the ones who had an undeniable air of the rodent about them. No matter how hard they tried to mask it, it was impossible. They kind of sidled in and out of places, rarely speaking. But when they did, more often than not, it was in a condescending tone of voice. They were easily pegged by the way they distanced themselves and crept around the fringes of the crowd. They'd slouch in a corner, trying to appear nonchalant in their aviator glasses, emitting a nervous, sweaty vibe. You could almost feel them listening in on conversations. Any hint of dirt seemed to make their ears grow.

The regulars at the station had great fun with these guys. The station was home to some of the greatest liars and bull-shit artists in the history of the world, and tabloid reporters were nothing more than a light snack before lunch for them. It was easy to reel the rats in with bits and pieces of made-up information and gossip thrown out in their vicinity. They'd twitch and their eyes would begin to gleam and they'd ease down the bar a bit. The locals would studiously ignore them and slightly turn their backs. All part of the plan. In a frantic attempt to appear uninterested, the rat-person would ask for a pickled egg or maybe order another beer. Working in groups of two or three, playing seamlessly off each other, the masters of the game would nudge the victim back onto the field with a hint that maybe a beer or two would keep them in their seats. The gears in rat-person's tiny brain would turn, weighing the price of setting up the house against getting an exclusive on the story of the century. Fame and fortune always won out and the drain on the rodent's expense account began. Great lies were told, punctuated with swear-to-gods and raised right hands. An occasional "Oh yeah, I seen it myself!" would be dropped into the conversation to be affirmed by a wave of nodding heads. An hour of this would cause great itching and trembling in the rat and a notebook would appear. Then someone would laugh. And then another and another. It would take a few minutes, but the rat would soon realize the joke was on him. He'd swell up like a toad, his lips would form a thin, hard line and he'd scuttle out of the station into the bright light of day to find another place to lurk. And then the evening would be filled with stories of how another intruder had been taken for a ride, then banished, by the local boys. The rodents were rare in those days; their type of reporting had not yet been legitimized. Then, the tactics they used were frowned upon.

The second of the four types were the new guys, fresh out of journalism school. They were easy to spot, too. Their blow-dried, razor-cut hair—sometimes highlighted just a hint—sparkled and shined in the south Georgia sun and was unadorned by a cap of any kind. I don't know if they all got together and decided on a uniform, but it seemed so. A uniform designed, I guess, to better blend in with the natives. Pressed khakis were popular, along with flannel shirts turned up, twice, at the cuff. Their work boots were only days out of the box and somehow stayed perpetually unscuffed. They ran everywhere, it seemed, and had an eagerness and sincerity about them that was damn-near painful. But it was still fun to watch the locals run these guys around in circles. And they soon learned not to ask directions from the beer drinkers who hung out around the station. The favorite joke was to send them miles out of their way along the back roads among the pine forests and fields. They'd return, hours later, with cockleburs clinging to their Velcro-pocketed vests and with their shininess dimmed a bit. I still see some of them from time to time as I click through the channels. And I laugh thinking about those who began their careers in Plains, learning the hard way not to try and match the local boys beer for beer at the bar.

And then there were the pros, a breed of people who always seemed to be rumpled and a bit weary but who had a way about them that made you glad you got to know them. They could fit in with any crowd, at once one of the boys and somehow strange and exotic at the same time. I think the most amazing thing about them, once I got to know them, was that they were just plain working people who, when on the road, worked their nine-to-five twenty-four hours a day. And they made friends easily, knowing that every day in a location may be their last. It was exciting to have these people in our town and it became a hobby of sorts to scan the papers every day and the weekly magazines trying to find articles written by people I knew. There was a brief period when I thought seriously about going into journalism and it was because of the pros. I wanted to be one of them; part of their club. I wanted a laminated press card to hang around my neck and the aura that went with it. Journalists carried with them then a weight, a responsibility, that everybody recognized. Especially the pros. And the ones I knew treated that responsibility with a certain respect. They seemed to know when not to see or hear things; when to keep things to themselves. They knew there was a time to be a beer-drinking buddy and a time to be a reporter. And they kept them separate. This was for their sake, too, because some of those guys could raise hell with the best of 'em. Some of my favorite memories are of now-major media figures drinking beer at the station bar, elbow to elbow with the regulars, totally engrossed in average, everyday conversations. And it is a credit to some of them that they've kept in touch through the years with the friends they made in town even after there were no more stories.

Of the four types of news people, the last are the worst. They are a strange mixture of the rodent and the pro. A particularly insidious group of people who, unfortunately, seem to be the ones who end up with all the attention. They are those who ease into false friendships, then rip you apart later down the road when it suits them best. Sometimes the backstabbing is a year or two in the making and becomes that much more of a shock when you realize the person writing the story about your family has been in your home and eaten dinner at your table. The second time brings with it the same shock and a little embarrassment at being so gullible. But the third and the fourth and all the times after are received with a cynicism that never goes away. There is one man, now at the top of his profession, who probably invented this category. He'd written a particularly nasty piece about the old man and his drinking after spending a few days at our house, enjoying our hospitality and my mother's cooking. Which would have been fine, really; it was nothing we hadn't read before by people we didn't know. But a few days before the article came out I'd helped this same guy back to his room after finding him facedown in his own vomit beside the swimming pool at the Best Western motel in Americus. He acted hurt and pretended not to understand why he was not welcomed when he came around again. I've often wondered how many people he fucked over to get where he is today. There were only four or five of these guys out of the hundreds who came through town. And they're all still in the business and all doing well. It is a mystery.

Most of the press who came to town seemed to have been everywhere and done everything. Plains, I think, was still a little bit of a shock to them. There was nothing for them to do there. So pretty much all of them ended up at the station. And ending up there meant there was no way they could avoid running into the old man.

I think there was a mild degree of surprise among the media when they realized the old man was not impressed with them. He didn't change at all when they were around; he did what he always did, which was drink beer and throw bullshit at anybody who walked through the door. If you could handle it, you were more than welcomed. If not, you could come in anyway but you had to be quiet and stay out of the way. Whatever the case, the press had found an ongoing show and it was my dad. I think some of them initially thought they'd uncovered an illiterate, semiretarded sibling of the maybe next president. They were sorely mistaken. Those who dismissed him as such quickly found themselves chewed up and spit out. He was more than their equal as far as matching wits and far superior with comebacks and put-downs. Some of his first enemies in the press were made at the station when some poor soul decided it was time the red-neck learned a lesson or two; time the backwoods idiot was put in his place. The old man loved it. The rest of us did, too, because I'll admit there was something strangely pleasing about watching some Yankee reporter being humiliated by one of our own. In the beginning my dad never asked for these pissing contests. There is an innate politeness that most people from small towns all across the country possess, and those of us from Plains are no different. So when ass-holes appeared in our midst they were initially treated just like the rest of the newcomers . . . until they showed their true personalities three, four, even five times. Everybody was treated with the same respect and given chances to return that respect. If you didn't, there was ample opportunity to figure out you weren't agreeable company. So if some reporter was blatant with his "aggressive journalism" with the old man, the first few times he would just be ignored and given the chance to go away. But if they continued, and they always did, the old man would turn his temper on them. They rarely tested him again. This is not to say he never met his match; he did. A few years after the press discovered him, he learned just how vicious some of them could be, and whatever charm and wit he possessed was nothing compared to the power they held.

But in the beginning it was strange and wonderful and flattering to have these people in our town. There was really no way not to be caught up in the excitement; it roamed the streets and walked through the doors. People new to us took an interest in our everyday, small-town, south Georgia lives. They brought with them attitudes and bits and pieces of things far removed from where we were. And as much fun as we made of the press badges and the cameras and the clothing and the personalities of the people who came with them, for a while at least, we were all secretly awed by them.

I think, too, some of them were charmed by the people and the pace of life in the area. There are a few who came, as temporary residents, who have since retired to Plains or one of the surrounding towns. It may be they felt they discovered something that is getting harder and harder to find in this country; places thought long gone or only read about or remembered from childhood.

But while all the attention was fun in the beginning, and there's no doubt we reveled in it, I wish there had been some kind of manual supplied with instructions on what it would do. Because it wasn't long after the first outsiders came that others followed.

And then the circus came to town.

Chapter Ten

And what a circus it was.

Imagine a town that meant little to anyone but its residents. A town ignored by those who passed through, considered nothing more than an annoyance because the speed limit dropped twenty miles an hour for a minute and a half. Some who traveled 280 on a regular basis may have thought of Plains as a milepost of sorts, indicating only a few more minutes to Americus or another hour's driving time to Columbus. Others might have glimpsed the fine, old homes on Main Street and the covered sidewalks along the storefronts and thought briefly of coming back at another time to explore our little town. But I imagine the name "Plains" soon vanished from their minds, even if they'd bothered to read the city limits sign in the first place.

Plains was not perfect by any stretch of the imagination. The term "the other side of the tracks" was a literal truth and still is. The town is divided by railroad tracks, and blacks live on one side and whites on the other. And obvious, pre-1960s racist attitudes still abound among some, even at the end of the century as they did throughout my childhood. But this is how we lived; how we were born and raised. There are people in my life, people close to me, who have lived those attitudes and perpetuated them. And as much as I would have liked to see them change, they never did and I loved them still. To dismiss them from my life would have been to deny the things in them that were good. It may seem horrible that I turned a blind eye and a deaf ear to the things I saw and heard as I was growing up: the deference paid by hardworking black farmers to some whites who weren't worth the time of day, or slurs and vile comments thrown about more often than not just for the shock value. But I did. And it is appalling to me now to think the reason I did was that it was easier than speaking up.

But in spite of that undertone threading its way through our town, on the surface, at least, Plains is a postcard come to life. It is hard for me not to have a soft spot in my heart for a place where there is real interest each summer in who is going to claim bragging rights for producing the first ripened tomato from their garden. A place where Halloween is celebrated each year at the Lion's Club Carnival, where old men in aprons and paper hats ladle Brunswick stew and barbecue and serve cornbread to a third of the population, while children, dressed in homemade costumes, bob for apples as they kneel around #2 washtubs. And there's the Garden Club and the Stitch & Chat, where ladies gather each month to, uh, stitch and, um, chat. And there is no escaping the impact of the churches. The week is planned around plays or revivals or potluck suppers. My mother spends a good part of each Saturday gleaning local gardens for flowers to grace the altar at Plains Maranantha Baptist Church. And I imagine children still give nickels and dimes each week in Sunday school, sealed in little paper envelopes, as offerings for the Lottie Moon missionaries. Vacation Bible School is a grand production, and each choir accepts with good grace the one or two members who sing off-key in praise of the Lord. Hours are spent on front porches fanning gnats from faces and slow rocking while winding down from the day. And, if you listen hard enough from the porch, you can maybe hear, from two blocks away, the tinkle of ice as your neighbor has one last glass of sweet tea before slipping through the screen door to retire for the night. Just imagine that.

Now try to imagine the sound of the clash when Plains met the rest of the world head-on. When Jimmy began gaining speed in his run for the White House, there was the natural inclination to find out where he came from. The press did this admirably and reported Plains and its inhabitants to the nation. And, for whatever odd reasons, people began to trickle in to experience the town for themselves. The first came and went with near-confused expressions on their faces at mistakenly expecting, I guess, some deep-south, kudzu-covered version of Disneyland. There were a few places then to purchase bumper stickers or T-shirts bearing grinning peanuts and such, but the serious speculators were still awaiting the November elections before flooding the town with piles of cheap plastic junk and everything from peanut butter ice cream to peanut butter pie. One everlasting lesson I learned from those days is that people will buy anything. *Anything.* No matter how useless or tasteless. And you don't even have to push them or advertise the product. If it's there, they will buy it. Sometimes, three or four of the *things* to carry back to Illinois or South Dakota to collect dust or to later take up space in the local landfill. But as I said, the first to come had nothing, really, to throw their money at. Some were disappointed; others were pissed off at trekking thirty miles off the interstate through flat land and pine forests to end up at a tiny spot on the map that didn't yet have, dammit, any souvenirs to buy. But a few knew what they'd found and actually idled a day or two away, soaking up an ambience they maybe felt, correctly as it turns out, was soon to disappear.

There's not much one can do with a tourist. The sport of gawking at them quickly grew tiresome when we realized they were gawking right back. The difference was we knew what we were doing; they, on the other hand, had no idea. It was a tourist thing. And I'll have to admit there was something mildly endearing about watching someone take Polaroids of a gas pump or seeing the looks of real disbelief on their faces when informed there was no Holiday Inn in town. And I quickly learned all things are relative. This lesson came as I sat in front of the station one day eating potted meat and soda crackers. An elderly gentleman and his wife pulled up in a Lincoln and got out to roam around a bit. They watched me for a while then asked what I was eating. I told them and offered a taste. Oh yes, they said, and I scooped some out with a cracker, carefully avoiding the bits of aorta. I was pretty amazed when they declared it the best thing they'd ever eaten. Even more so when they left with our entire supply of potted meat, just as happy as hell. As they pulled out, I could see the wife daintily extracting a Vienna sausage from one of the four cans they bought after I'd promised them that "potted meat ain't shit compared to these things."

The number of tourists in Plains grew with every primary Jimmy won. At first there were only ten or fifteen a day; then a few dozen. They were a great diversion for a while, and we kept up with license plates and marveled that a carload of folks from Washington state or Minnesota might find us interesting. By the time a hundred or more a day came through, though, the newness had waned a good bit and a lot of us were thinking that, surely, this is enough. We had no idea.

We all had our own lives to live and became like stones in the stream of tourists flowing into town. The old man at this time hadn't yet been in the spotlight a good deal so there was really no draw to the station except its cool, dim interior and its cold, cold beer. There were two definite types of travelers to darken the doorway. The first were the family folks, with children in tow. Station wagons would pull up to the pumps and a crowd would spill out. We were full-service then: filling the tank, washing the windshield, checking the oil. So there was ample opportunity for the dad to fire questions at us. Where's Jimmy? they would ask, as if he might be inside sucking down a cold one. By reflex, because they always asked, directions to Jimmy's house were given. You'd throw your arm out, pointing down 280 west and say: "Twoblocksdownlookforthebiggateonyourrightcan'tmissit." They'd nod, lay their gaze on Main Street, then ask, "What's there to do around here?" Which was always answered with a shrug and a "Not much." Another nod and then they'd take the first tentative steps through the front door.

Sometimes the dads would let their eyes linger on the bar and the sweat beading on the cold cans and bottles slammed down in front of the locals. Others quickly gathered their children around them and huddled in the corner nearest the door, waiting for their change, before bustling out and crossing 280 for the safety of Main Street. A few just peeped through the door and chose to wait outside for change. The peeping was often accompanied by the flash of an Instamatic. I've wondered if the pictures were used as props as they told tales back home of their brush with danger and a close encounter with honest-to-God good ol' boys.

Others who came to the station entered and didn't leave for hours. The place had the universal feel of the hangout about it, and these folks knew a good place when they found it. In the next few years, some even set aside a day or two of their annual vacations to visit and drink beer.

I don't know the exact moment it happened, but sometime during the period Jimmy was winning primaries, the old man became "Billy Carter." The press already knew about him, but then he was just the brother, the guy who took care of the family business and owned the local beer joint. He wasn't seen often; there was a warehouse to run, and the old man didn't spend that much time at the station—maybe an hour or two a day and maybe a little more on weekends. I can only imagine it was in their boredom that the press "discovered" him. When Jimmy came home for a day or two, the press stayed close to Plains and the station was a natural attraction to a good many of them. It is not hard to figure how a Friday night of drinking beer and eating catfish there, with the old man as host, could quickly bring him to their attention. Many Pabst Blue Ribbons brought out the best bullshit in the old man, and twenty or thirty near-stoned journalists made for a fine audience. It wasn't long before pictures of him with a can in front of his face began appearing in newspapers all over the country. He was described as "earthy" or "colorful," meaning he wasn't afraid to cuss in public, or as a "character." I look at some of those old clippings now and can see a wariness in his eyes mixed with a certain shyness. And I can tell from those first pictures he wasn't quite as comfortable with all the attention as some may have thought he was.

Whatever the case, after he'd told a few people to kiss his ass, drunk twenty-seven beers at a sitting, then proclaimed himself to be a Wallace Democrat, all in front of the press, he became some kind of blue-collar folk hero; a sort of anti-Jimmy that appealed to the workers and wage earners around the country. It wasn't long before someone in Jimmy's campaign, or maybe Jimmy himself, realized the old man could be an asset, and he was sent out to try and pull in a few votes. He was a hit. This was no surprise to me or the rest of the family;

we'd known for years how he was with a crowd.

My dad was two different people. No . . . three. Hell, he was a lot more than that but only three I would dare try and define. One was the guy we saw at home; the one who provided for us and disciplined us. The man who read four newspapers a day and seven or eight novels a week and who could discuss any topic from how much rain was needed to make a crop to global politics. Another was the man who worked hard every day in the family business, putting 100 percent of his attention to the task. A man respected by the people who did business with him and the ones who worked for him.

The third was the man the press paid attention to. There's no blame being laid on anyone here; this third man was the most interesting and made for the best stories. And this was the man they saw at the station relaxing for an hour or two at the end of the day. The showman, the man quick, *quick*, with a comeback, who cussed and raised hell and drank beer. He was quotable. Sometimes embarrassingly so. But in the beginning this was okay, it was harmless. We *all* enjoyed it, even the people on the barbed end of his wit. Even so, I think his outrageousness was a defense mechanism of sorts; there was no way he was going to show fear in front of some Yankee reporter. He'd always been a fighter and contrary as hell, and if he lacked sense in anything it was in knowing when to back down. If he was accused of drinking too much in public or saying things he shouldn't have said, it only served to fuel the fire and for him to double his efforts. *Nobody* was going to tell the old man how to act.

But, as I said, it was harmless at first. It was all like chapter one in a fairy tale. If someone had told the old man a year earlier that one day he would be a nationally known figure, I'm sure he would have laughed. If anyone in town had been told that as many as ten thousand tourists a day would soon be roaming the streets, they would have been called crazy. So, of course, he was taken with the attention. Of course he was flattered. I think it is impossible for anyone not to be. I was a teenager and suddenly my old man became synonymous with partying and hellraising. Cool. It was *all right* to be pointed out as one of the Carters and to be questioned about what it was like. For a while, at least, I was eaten up all to hell with it. And damn-near the whole town was giddy with the experience.

When I look back now, it is easy to peg those first few months as the beginning of all the old man's future problems. Being that the press rarely saw him outside of the atmosphere of the station, it's no surprise that most of the pictures taken were of him holding a beer. Tourists wanted to be able to say they bought him a Pabst and he accommodated them. There were times when he raised a can to his lips, that the room would light up from the flashbulbs going off, and everything he said was scribbled down in a notebook. Before long, his time at home grew shorter and shorter as he amused and entertained down at the station. He had fans now, and he gave them what they wanted. He gave them Billy Carter. Nobody knew, then, that the bear was out and there was no way in hell anybody was going to get him back in.

There came a time when the station was no longer a refuge for my dad. The number-one question of "Where's Jimmy live?" was replaced by "Where's Billy?" It seemed everyone wanted an autograph or a picture taken with him. Others just wanted some of his time to sit and talk and drink a beer. Some came with problems they thought only he could understand and help them with by his access to Jimmy. I never saw him push anyone away or deny anyone a picture or a word or two. At least none of the tourists. The tabloid presses, the rodents, were another story. He would not tolerate them and avoided them whenever they were around. And he became pretty damn good at slipping away from both the press and the tourists whenever he felt like it. There were many, many days when Bud Duvall would pick up the old man at the warehouse and they would hit the old roads away from Plains and the crowds. I asked Bud if they talked about what was going on in town and was surprised to learn it was very rarely mentioned. Instead, they rode like they always did, checking out the fields and the farms; stopping every now and then to talk to friends or to rummage in the cooler in the truck bed for another beer. I doubt if either of them ever thought that those particular escapes away from Plains were some of the last. They had no way of knowing that what was happening back in town, and to the old man, was just a mere hint of what was to be. Nobody knew that the town, my dad, my family—hell, everything and everybody in any way connected—was on its way to becoming a very strange, very bizarre reflection of what it once was.

Sign on Main Street, covered the day after Billy died

Billy and Jimmy growing up

James Earl Carter, Sr., the grandfather

Billy in high school . . .

. . . and soon after as a young Marine

Sybil and Billy's wedding photo

Billy Carter and those famous Georgia peanuts

Carolyn Carter

Plains, Georgia, 1976

Art Seitz

Typical day at the gas station—Billy and Buddy at left

On the plane, headed for the Inauguration

Buddy Carter

One more press conference, one more beer

Billy Beer Day in Plains

Buddy Carter

Buddy's sister Jana, and Billy in front of the pretentious Christmas tree

Buddy Carter

World Cannon Ball and Billy Flop Contest in Vancouver, B.C.

A typical Billy Carter stance

Playing the media game with "Smokin' Joe" Frazier

Billy and Sybil—a lifetime together

Chapter Eleven

The old man hit the campaign trail. And the people who handled him, to the extent they *could* handle him, knew exactly what to do with him. No speeches; no policy or platform talks. He went to the bars and the taverns, talking to the people who looked at him as one of them. He told jokes Billy Carter-style, cussed the government, talked about farming or whatever else crossed his mind, and drank a lot of beer and bourbon. The crowds at bigger campaign events crowded around and closed him in to touch or talk to the man closest to Jimmy, the big dog. Some came just to see the old man, telling him there was no way in hell they'd vote for his brother. "But man," they'd say, "you're just like us. You keep tellin' 'em what you think!" And they'd laugh and shake his hand or slap him on the back. There was something about him that reminded people of their crazy brother-in-law or wayward uncle. He made them comfortable; he made them laugh.

Apparently, those who ran the primary campaigns in each state had been warned about him. And the old man knew it. He had a knack for skating right to the edge of controversy and used it often. There was generally someone at each location who was assigned the job of taking care of the old man and keeping him out of trouble. The problem was that the Billy-sitter, more often than not, was a nineteen- or twenty-year-old political science major from a local university or college who had no idea what they'd volunteered for. Those who didn't try to treat him like a South Georgia redneck usually ended up having a pretty good time with some damn good stories to tell. Stories, I imagine, that won hands down against any others told back at the fraternity house. But if the handler started the relationship trying to show the old man who was boss or made the mistake of waving a college degree at him, they were handed two or three days of pure hell. Not that my dad was mean or malicious towards these people. He would just disappear. There is nothing like watching the person "in charge" frantically trying to find their ward fifteen minutes before a scheduled campaign event. Especially if said ward is the brother of the probable next Democratic Party candidate for president of the United States. Most of the time the old man could be found at a bar having one hell of a time or a block or two down the street shooting the shit with some of the locals in the hardware store.

Another trick was for him to tell the handler all the things he was going to say to the press when they arrived; awful things about race and the environment and welfare and such. He would go into great detail about how he didn't think Jimmy was quite up to speed on these issues and how he was going to clear things up for him. The handler would laugh nervously as if he was quite sure he was being kidded; then when the old man kept talking, there would be clandestine phone calls to headquarters begging for help. And then the local press would arrive for the interview, and every time the old man drew a breath to speak the handler would wince and cringe as if waiting for his career to end before it even started. By the time the interviews were over, the guy in charge was pale and exhausted, yet relieved that the old man didn't carry through with his threat. The handler was usually so grateful that the remainder of my father's stay was pretty much enjoyable. This holding back, though, lasted only a year or so after he entered the limelight. He later grew into the habit of saying exactly whatever the hell was on his mind.

But he enjoyed that first campaign. And I think he was amazed a bit that people wanted to be around him and hear what he had to say. There was still a shyness and a graciousness about him that first time around. There was a playfulness that seemed to rub off on anybody that came into contact with him. And he was never boring, which always made his arrival in town worth a front-page story. I don't know how much difference he made in the first campaign. Some will tell you he brought in a lot of votes; others wished he'd just stayed home. I *do* know he developed a taste for fame on those trips. And the odd thing was how easily he seemed to slip into the game.

I went on a few of those campaign trips with him, just to tag along. At that point in my life, I was fifteen; I'd never been much farther than Panama City Beach, so it was a great experience for me. There was great excitement in the headquarters of the winning candidate; a buzz that is hard to describe; an energy you can't help absorbing. The one thing I remember most from those trips, that had nothing at all to do with the campaign, was when we were in Green Bay, Wisconsin. I'd gone with the old man and a group of people who were part of the "Peanut Brigade"—volunteers, mostly from Georgia, who paid their own way to go and campaign for Jimmy. My father, Jimmy, and I were in a small room at the campaign headquarters. My dad had just called home to check in with my mother. When he hung up, there were tears in his eyes. He looked at me and said, "Sheba died." Sheba was the family dog who'd terrorized Plains for ten years or more and hated everybody but my sisters and me. She'd bitten my dad more than once and had been known to eat a Chihuahua on occasion. But before I knew it, both my old man and Jimmy were crying. I cried, too, because I was the kid and my dog was gone. I don't think Sheba would have cried for the old man or Jimmy, though. She didn't like either of them.

There was something about Jimmy's first campaign for the presidency that met all the requirements for becoming a bona fide "special" thing. In Plains, at least, where that great blanket of cynicism and weariness hadn't yet fogged us in, there was a feeling that *anything* was possible. At times, it seemed the whole town was somehow involved in the campaign, from stuffing envelopes to displaying that famous Southern hospitality all the visitors expected. We were all celebrities, part of a living, breathing political phenomenon, and those who chose to join in put 100 percent into playing their parts. Those who didn't had the good grace to stay out of the way, and some clustered together in little groups at the local café, bitching and moaning and sniping and complaining. The old train depot, abandoned for years, was cleaned up and painted and converted into the "Official Jimmy Carter for President National Campaign Headquarters." My grandmother received visitors there several times a week while sitting in a big, old rocking chair beneath the covered porch. She'd already been introduced to the world through the press and had become a star herself. She was sharp-tongued and witty and not shy at all about saying whatever was on her mind. Tourists would approach her and shyly shake her hand and speak a word or two. Depending on her mood, Grandma could either be the most gracious lady in the world or just meaner than hell. And having been snapped at by Miss Lillian became a badge of sorts the tourists proudly wore.

I think one of my favorite Grandma stories involves the time she was visited at the Pond House by a reporter. It was a scheduled visit but she was still a little irate at having to put up with him. Maybe there was a ball game in progress, or one of her "stories," and she didn't appreciate the interruption. Whatever the case, the reporter was there to question her about Jimmy making the statement in one of his stump speeches that he would never lie to the American public. He later said that maybe he'd told a few white lies in his time, but nothing major. The reporter wanted to know the difference between a white lie and a full-blown lie. "Well," my grand-mother told the reporter, "a white lie is like when I just opened the door and said I was happy to see you." I can't imagine the interview getting any better after that.

When I look back on those first days, the days when the campaign became real and it looked as though Jimmy was going to win the nomination, I can't help equating what was going on in Plains to a Little Rascals' "Gee, let's put on a show"-type atmosphere. The air snapped with energy and excitement and the feeling that great things were on the way. The town swarmed with strange and wonderful people who wanted to experience the place that could maybe produce a president. The press picked up on the genuine charm of the locals and reported it to the country. And this charm became an asset to the campaign. So much so that it was exported in the form of the "Peanut Brigade," the group of supporters who spent their money and their time traveling the primary states. They became a common sight, these farmers and teachers, these everyday people, dressed in green and white, clacking and clanging from all the buttons covering their clothing, boarding buses to go forth and preach the gospel of Jimmy. And it worked. There's no doubt these true believers

made a difference. Farmers in New Hampshire are no different from farmers in Georgia; the language is the same.
And I think a lot of people were impressed with the heart
displayed by the Peanut Brigade; these Southern-fried folks
would stand for hours in the snow on a street corner up
north somewhere, speaking for their favorite son. It was a
fine example of a true grassroots movement.

The change in my father during that spring and summer of
1976 was not a big one, but it was there. He was getting
almost as much attention as Jimmy at the time, something I
think he liked more than he let on. And of course he was
excited, just like the rest of us. But first and foremost on his
mind every morning when he woke up was the warehouse, the
same way it had been for years. I don't think any amount of
celebrity could have taken him away from the business. The
tourists and the press and all the weird stuff going on around
town were a source of amusement for him, a hobby of sorts.
The Billy Carter found at the station at the end of the day and
the Billy Carter running the family business were not at all
alike. And I think if people outside of those who knew him
best could have somehow seen them side by side, they would
have sworn they were talking to two different men.

But it was the station Billy that people most wanted to talk
to. He was the one who made them laugh, the one who made
for the best print, the best sound bites. And though he gave
them what they wanted, I know he grew tired of it pretty
quickly. I can't count the Saturday afternoons, when things at
the station were just heating up, just getting to the beginning
of five or six hours of beer drinking and hell raising, that he
would leave a lot earlier than normal. He would walk out the
door, grinning and joking, and sign a few autographs and pose
for a few pictures. But when he turned away to walk back
behind the station to his truck, the grin would fall from his

face and his shoulders would slump. The few times I broke away from the crowd to catch up with him, he told me he was going home or maybe to ride a while. I know he was concerned about what was happening to the town; he'd said so many times. But I've wondered a lot if, even then, he wasn't concerned about what was happening to him. Not the drinking, because it hadn't yet become the problem that eventually took over his life. He was at a point where things finally seemed to be going well for him. The business was doing very well, something that could be directly attributed to his management. He had the station, a place he and his friends could gather and have good times. The family was fine and about to have a new addition. All was well, it seemed.

But I wonder if my father somehow sensed, in those early days, that things would never again be the same for him. Oh, he knew that if Jimmy were elected president his life would be different. There was no escaping that. But I'd always thought there were a hundred different directions for my dad to choose from; a hundred different ways he could handle his celebrity. And then I find myself thinking that maybe *he* was not the one who was going to decide anything. The town itself was already miles and miles away from where it began only months before, to say nothing of its inhabitants. And short of barricading 280 and all the county roads leading to Main Street there was nothing anybody could do about it. What was happening was well beyond anybody's control. It was like weather—you just sat back and watched the rain. The old man, I think, figured this out a long time before anybody else did and resigned himself to it. I guess he could have raised hell and refused interviews or completely changed his personality when the press was around. Maybe then he would have been ignored as just one of 250 million others roaming the country. Maybe it would have been best for everybody if the very first time he walked into the station and found a guy standing there with a pencil in one hand and a notebook in the other he turned and ran the other way. But then he would not have been my old man. He wouldn't have been the guy people had grown to expect to throw his personality full-force into whatever situation arose. And I think he would have considered it an unnatural act to try and be anything other than what he was.

While my dad may have figured out early on that a big change for him personally was on its way, what he thought and how he felt about it he kept to himself. This was not unusual; he had never been a person to have deep conversations with anyone, much less his family. Other than sensing a vague dis-quiet about him from time to time, I don't think anybody noticed that much of a difference in him. There was too much going on, too much to see. I never thought to take the time to study what was happening in our lives. And it never occurred to me in those moments that there could be a downside to the ride we'd just begun. I was part of the *family* and I loved it. Hell, I was on the bus; I was with the band. For a sixteen-year-old boy who'd grown up in Plains, Georgia, this was *it*. I'd been given a gift, it seemed: the key to the candy store. Places tourists couldn't go *I* was welcomed. "Aw, hell, that's Billy's son," I'd hear time and again. "He's all right. Let him in." The old man's inner circle was wide open to me, and I could slip in and sit quietly and soak up everything that went along with being one of the boys, a member of the club. It wasn't until a few years later, though, that I realized I was also a gatekeeper of sorts. Just one of many who formed an informal buffer between my old man and the outsiders invading our territory. Everyone who spent a lot of time at the station, I think, dis-played a kind of loyalty towards him and protected him to some degree. It is strange for me, even now, to think of him as one who needed protection from anything or anybody, but he did. I know now, even though he would have never allowed it, that maybe we should have spent more effort trying to protect him from himself. But, again, there was too much happening for me to want to take the time to spend worrying about my father. I had developed an attitude of my own by then, an attitude that became painfully obvious to me only after those days were over.

If the attention we received during the primaries surprised us, the few days before and those following the nomination damn near blew us away. Jimmy came back to Plains to interview potential candidates for vice president, and the big dogs with the press followed him. It became pretty common to see famous, nightly news personalities broadcasting from the sidewalk on Main Street or on the corner in front of Jimmy's house. The Secret Service was with him by this time and gave us all something else to gawk at or talk about. Jimmy's motorcade alone was impressive as hell with about fifty cars barreling down 280, half of which had lights flashing. And then the national press broadcast live from Main Street the night of the nomination, and thousands of people came to help celebrate. And they kept coming. It was all a true, honest-to-God, once-in-a-lifetime sight to see.

The days of dogs sleeping in the streets were over.

Chapter Twelve

Jimmy was elected president of the United States.

The celebration the night of the election was the single most exciting thing I had ever experienced in my life. It has been estimated that a couple of hundred thousand people crowded into Plains that night. I know for a fact that cars lined both sides of 280 for up to three miles in either direction of town and were parked in any available space within the city limits. A huge stage was built on Main Street and big screens were erected so everyone could watch the returns, and there were bright lights mounted everywhere. There were bands playing and speakers speaking, and the noise rolled from the streets of town all the way to the peanut fields and pine forests on the outskirts. I don't remember moments exactly, there were too many and each as intense as the next. I spent most of that night back and forth between downtown, swimming the ocean of people, and our house, which became more crowded by the minute. It was strange, walking the once-quiet streets I'd spent most of my life traveling. That night they were filled with strangers overflowing from the main crowd. What was once a ten-minute stroll became a half-hour struggle. True to form, the old man had found the ultimate excuse for a party and he did himself proud. The porch was lined with kegs of beer and there were uncountable bottles of liquor. So many people filled our yard that I knew there was no way Mama could lay her Mama-eyes upon me, and I snagged a few beers whenever the crowd parted in front of the kegs. And then a few more when I made my way back downtown. This was all great fun for several hours. But there came a moment when I didn't like it anymore. The party at our house became more of an invasion than a celebration. I remember a great feeling of unease coming over me when I entered the house late that night and found every room packed with people, and they were all drunk. I didn't know *anybody*. I was at *home* and I couldn't find a familiar face anywhere, and I wanted to go to bed. But the old man had opened his arms and welcomed in anyone who trickled down to that end of town. I don't know where he was but Mama suddenly appeared and, after finding a complete stranger asleep in her bed, began to run people off. She was scared for Earl, my little brother, who was only a month old at the time. One guy asked her who the hell she thought she was. He left immediately after. We all accepted what my dad had done; we didn't know any other way. In true Billy Carter fashion, he'd gone the extreme route, not once, I think, even wondering what he'd created. Looking back, I view that one party as an omen of sorts of what the next few years of life with my old man were going to be like: fun at times, confusing and scary at others. Where he ended up that night I don't know. I do know that wherever he was, he was at the center of it all, twelve hours into a three-day, blind-running drunk. He could be forgiven, though. It's not every day your brother is elected president. And everybody was pulling at him that night. The country had only seen a little bit of the old man and they wanted more. And election night 1976 made for the perfect backdrop.

The next day was more of the same. Except for early that morning. I left home to walk to the station and check any damage that may have been done. What I saw when I walked out the front door and made my way down the back streets was one of the eeriest things I'd ever seen. At first I thought there were hundreds of dead people curled up in the yards. Then I realized they were all just sleeping off the party from the night before. It reminded me of the scene from *Gone With the Wind* when the camera pulled back to show all the dead and dying lying together after the battle. I could hear faint moans and occasionally someone would rise to a sitting position and wobble for a while. People wandered up and down Main Street, through the trash and debris, with dazed looks on their faces. Fortunately, the old man had seen there was no way the station could handle the crowd and had closed early the day before. Otherwise, I think the place would have been destroyed. As it was, cleaning up took twice as long as normal, counting the interruptions of people rapping on the windows begging for a little hair of the dog or desperately searching for a packet of Goody's headache powders. It was strange to look out over the town in that hour or so before the crowd gathered again. If I ignored the trash and squinted a bit to blur the sight of the huge stage, Plains still looked like Plains. I know it wasn't, though. Not really. And it is still hard to believe that a town that sometimes appeared on maps of the state and sometimes didn't was host to the biggest party South Georgia had ever seen.

That party appeared to be the beginning of good times, *great* times, for the old man. When Jimmy stood on that giant stage and gave his victory speech, he thanked my father. Without

Billy taking care of the business, he said, he never could have gone into politics in the first place. Mama tells me that was one of the best moments of my father's life. Acknowledgment, finally, of a job well done. Acknowledgment he'd worked for; acknowledgment he'd earned. And it could not have meant any more to him than it did coming from his brother.

My dad's own business, the station, was sure to do well. The election guaranteed that. If the tourist trade in the months before the election, months when it appeared Jimmy just *might* be president, were any indication of what was going to be, then the station was a bona fide gold mine.

And then there was all the attention the old man himself was receiving. Offers were coming in for him to go and be himself on talk shows and store openings and other events. They wanted him to be Billy Carter—sharp tongue, quick wit, beer can in hand and all. And they wanted to pay him for it, for God's sake.

It would have been easy for him to go wild, much wilder than he already was, when all this began. And I don't know just how much he was tempted. But the one big constant in his life, the family business, was still there and he was still in charge. Crops still grew and needed to be processed. That was the one thing in his life that wouldn't change. Or at least no one thought so.

I still admire the way my dad handled his overnight fame— and it *was* virtually overnight—when it first found him. He went about most of his days the way he always had. If he changed at all, it was hard to tell. Things seemed to go a little easier for us at home. Every day there was some new thing to talk about: gift shops opening up, a celebrity newsperson, weird and strange tourist stories. The old man gave newspaper and magazine interviews and did some TV stuff. My sisters and I devoured it all and became his biggest fans. We'd cluster together in front of the screen cheering him on and half-disbelieving we were seeing our dad. We were proud of him. He was funny and charming and he held his own against some of the best in the business. We were unaware then he was on his way to becoming a true "personality." He was still just our dad. Other times we'd read things about him in the tabloids and laugh out loud. Even then they were trying desperately to find something scandalous in the way the old man conducted himself. Most of the time they created things. By now everyone in town had learned to detect the aura of sleaze around the tabloid guys and pretty much shunned them. At first some of the things we read really pissed us off, but we learned very quickly we'd be in a constant state of irritation if we paid too much attention to what was written. I didn't know it then, but that lesson was just the first of many, many thin layers of veneer we were coated with that would eventually become a thick, hard shell. A shell all of us had to wear as protection from the shit storm headed our way.

Any kind of trouble, though, was the last thing on our minds. We were going to Washington, D.C., by God. A Carter was to be sworn in as president of the United States. There were plans to make and tuxedos to rent. And while we were waiting for the inauguration, Plains was changing right before our eyes. Main Street was transformed into a combination of the strip at Panama City Beach, Florida, and Victory Drive in Columbus. Or so it seemed to me. I sure as hell never expected I'd see a souvenir shop in town, but within days of the election there were several. A quick trip down the sidewalk in front of our postcard-perfect business district, along with a pocket full of cash, could get you all of the cheap, plastic, foreign-made things you could ever care to own. There were Jimmy T-shirts, Jimmy caps, Jimmy buttons, and Jimmy bumper stickers. If you needed Jimmy mugs and Jimmy keychains or maybe a plastic Jimmy bottle opener made in the shape of his head with giant teeth sticking out, they were all easily found. There were eight-by-ten, glossy color photographs of Jimmy and plates with his painted profile. Jimmy towels, Jimmy ties and Jimmy socks. Of course, you had your Jimmy jewelry and your Jimmy pencils, pens and pads. Jimmy coloring books were popular, as well as Jimmy snow globes that featured a little tiny plastic Jimmy standing beside an even tinier peanut. And then there was the tacky stuff. The things manufactured by people who I am sure have their very own special place reserved in Hell. I won't list them all, they are too numerous. But my favorites, those being the most hideous, were the little blue boxes labeled "Hillbilly Toilet Paper" that contained a corn cob, and "Electric Hillbilly Toilet Paper," a corn cob with an electrical cord attached to one end. Stop it, you're killing me. Sometimes I try to imagine the brainstorming session that gave birth to those products. Then I stop, fearful I might find myself rubbing my chin and saying out loud, "Hmm, I understand." Even more amazing was the fact they couldn't keep the things on the shelves.

Hungry? Main Street Plains had peanuts: raw, roasted, boiled, brittled, fried, pied and liquefied. If you didn't want to eat them you could buy kits to grow them yourself or buy a book to read about them. There were peanut pins for your lapel and cartoon peanuts with teeth painted on them. You could spend your money on peanut wreaths or peanuts adorned with pipe cleaners and little, plastic googly eyes. And mixed in with all the Jimmy, Plains, and peanut memorabilia were the brightly colored, plastic things found in every cheesy souvenir shop in the country—from curly straws to cheap sunglasses.

The old man made a real effort in the beginning to try and keep Main Street from becoming just another tacky little tourist trap. His voice was drowned out by all the others screaming that he was being greedy and only wanted to keep all the money for himself. That was laughable. More tourists visited the station than all the other places in town combined. He could have sold all the plastic things he wanted, hundreds of thousands of plastic things, but chose instead to stick with beer, which he'd always sold, and T-shirts.

There was a real war going on in town at that time. A war between those who wanted to take things slow and easy, and maybe maintain a little dignity about the whole thing, and those who wanted money and, goddammit, wanted it right now. I found it interesting that a lot of those who bitched about Jimmy and the Carters in the first place were not shy at all about profiting off his name. And I never understood how some of the more pious in town, the ones who tsk-tsked the old man's beer drinking, somehow justified screwing the tourists in their own places of business. I'm not condemning anyone for wanting to make a little money. It was practically lining the streets in those days anyway, flying out of the tourists' pockets. A person couldn't help wanting to grab up a handful for himself. But, damn, it was ugly.

The town folks weren't the only ones who realized there was a buck to be made. People from as far away as California rented space on Main Street and opened businesses. Notice I say "rented." These guys were pros and knew better than to sink a bunch of money into something that could disappear in four years. I later found out this strange breed of entrepreneur kept up with all the hot spots and places in the news around the country and moved accordingly, rushing into a town with a couple of gallons of paint and a few boxes of goods. A lot of the money made in Plains didn't stay there. It left in the pockets of those temporary residents.

And it was good for a while to see all that activity in town. Everyday, with the streets crowded, was reminiscent of past

Saturday nights on Main Street. There were no more empty buildings. Even the alley behind all the businesses was filled with little souvenir or snack shops. But while you could find all the Chinese backscratchers or cones of peanut ice cream you needed, locating a loaf of bread or a can of soup became a quest.

It is easy now for me to look back and criticize; to rant and rave about the attitude my town developed. But then I find myself more forgiving. The years have cleared things up a bit. In those early days, it seems, everyone was infected with the desire to grab their piece of the action. Who could blame us? We were all taken with the attention. Plains seemed to be the center of the universe. Nobody asked for the tourists to appear and wave their money around. *They* came to *us*. And we accommodated them. Not always tastefully, but we gave them what they wanted. And it is pointless now to think about how the opportunity the town was given was quickly exhausted, wrung dry. That opportunity is gone now.

It's hard to imagine the sheer number of people who made their way to Plains during the four years Jimmy was in office. It is estimated that as many as ten thousand a day stopped by. And most of those visited the station. Prior to those days, it was nothing to play an uninterrupted game of rummy or read the entire *Atlanta Constitution* before being summoned to the gas pumps for a fill-up. Two people were all it took to keep the place running, and that's only if there was the occasional oil change or flat tire. Soon, though, there were six full-time positions at the station, two behind the bar and four out at the pumps. The line of cars waiting for gas snaked out onto 280. Twice-weekly beer deliveries became twice-daily, and we added a walk-in cooler to keep up with the demand. There was a constant stream of cases from the cooler in back to those up front. A second door was added behind the bar just so employees could enter and reach the cash register without having to wedge their way through the crowd packing the place. There were two public restrooms, accessible from outside, and one inside for the employees and the regulars. Tourists started to use the one inside. Before long, a hand-lettered sign appeared on the door. "WARNING!!" the sign said. "Growling Crotch Crickets!! Enter at Own Risk!!" It's not that anyone minded the tourists using our restroom. But it *was* comical to watch a person approach the door and place his hand on the knob. The sign would catch his eye and then he'd slowly back away and leave in search of another place to go. Others hesitantly turned the knob to peer around the open door. Some entered, some didn't. I don't remember anyone ever questioning the sign, though. I think some were more afraid of appearing ignorant in front of a bunch of good ol' boys than they were of the strange and horrible growling crotch crickets.

Though I knew the station to be a special place, it is still amazing to me that someone from far away would want to spend any time there. But some came to town only to sit at the bar and have a beer. They knew what the station was and didn't bother crossing 280 to Main Street. Connoisseurs, so to speak, of honky-tonks and roadside beer joints. Any given morning would find a person from clear across the country settling onto a barstool to become one of the boys for the day. We once had a couple from South Africa spend an entire week at the station, drinking beer with the boys and placing orders for barbecue when lunch time rolled around. These hard-core drinkers came from everywhere: Germany, Japan, Australia, Great Britain. They were a different breed from the other tourists, and it is curious that they were the ones who never seemed to bother the old man much. They just wanted to drink and soak up a little bit of atmosphere.

Along with the camera-toting tourists and the serious beer

drinkers, Plains drew another type of soul. Crazy people, to be blunt. Some were only mildly strange, the "that boy just ain't right" kind. And there were those weird enough to leave you with a vague feeling of uneasiness, who you were glad to see leave. But others gloried in their insanity and felt they should share it with the rest of the world. Of course, there was always a ready and willing audience at the station. An audience that didn't mind nurturing and egging on the crazy people. There were many of them, but three come to mind immediately. I call them Money Man, Weather Man, and Nasty Man.

Money Man looked like a banker. He was in his late fifties or early sixties and dressed very well in a suit with a tie and a black overcoat. There was nothing about him appearance-wise, really, that would distinguish him from anyone else. The first time I saw him was early one morning when I opened the station. I found him sitting on the bench out front with a large, brown paper bag in his lap. He said he didn't need anything from inside and after a while got up and walked to the end of the block. Then he turned around and walked to the other end. Then again. And again. He walked back and forth in front of the station for two hours holding his paper bag. Finally he stopped and came inside and bought a Coke. When he finished it, he got up and started walking again, back and forth. This continued all day, with periodic breaks, until the sun went down and he left. He was back the next morning, as genial as the day before, holding his brown paper grocery bag. Again he walked. Jimmy was in town at the time and someone made mention of the man with the bag to the Secret Service. The man wasn't causing any problems, he was just acting strangely, but one of the agents approached him and asked if they could talk to him for a moment. "Certainly," the man replied, so they took him to an office to ask a few questions. "Do you mind if we look in your bag?" they asked. "By all means," he said. Inside, they found sixty-three thousand dollars in twenties and hundreds. It was his. He never explained why he withdrew his entire life savings, put it in a paper bag, and then left Illinois to wander the streets of Plains, Georgia. His daughter was contacted and she flew down to get him. She apologized a lot for her father when she arrived. There was no need. He'd been polite to a fault and never bothered a soul.

Weather Man seemed to be from central casting. He was tall and thin and about seventy years old. His hair was cut in a waxed flat-top and he wore Converse tennis shoes, pants that were three inches too short, a white long-sleeved shirt, black suspenders, and a red bow tie. The glasses he wore had thick lenses set in black horn-rimmed frames. He looked as though he hadn't smiled in years. He walked into the station one Saturday afternoon carrying a clear plastic box in his arms, about eighteen inches square. Suspended by a thread in the box was a red ball of yarn that looked like a pom-pom off a knitted cap. We'd gotten over seeing strange-looking people by this time; tourists come in all shapes, sizes and varieties, but this guy definitely drew a few double takes. I could see grins spreading on the faces of a few of the locals. Fresh meat; free entertainment had entered. The man put the box on the bar and scowled at us. We silently watched the pom-pom swing back and forth, waiting for an explanation. None came and the tension grew damn-near unbearable. Finally, someone had to ask what the box was for. A mild look of disgust for all the ignorance in the room appeared on the man's face and he scowled some more before speaking. "It's a weather machine," he spat through clenched teeth, as if it hurt him to tell. "I'm here to make it rain." Everyone agreed we needed rain. Could he please, *please*, show us how it was done? He glared around the room again, trying to catch a smile, I guess, then nodded his head. I don't think anyone in the room was breathing as Weather Man bent over at the waist, placed his hands on his knees and peered at the pom-pom. He pursed his lips. "Woooooo. Woooooo," he said. Then again. "Woooooo. Woooooo." No one spoke. We couldn't. Weather Man straightened and walked out the door. He stood there for a while looking up at the sky then came back in. "Goddamn government," he said. "They know I'm here. Got their goddamn government planes parked overhead blockin' my machine. They do it every time." The station was full of people, including the old man, but no one was capable of a comeback; there was nothing anyone *could* say. But after a few moments of stunned silence, I heard from one of the regulars, "Try it again. Maybe them planes have moved by now." Weather Man visited twice more in the next few years, still shadowed by those government planes.

I guess it was the redneck/good ol' boy persona the old man wore for the press that made people feel comfortable around him. He wore it well and the public embraced him. It was harmless. But some took his act to be real and would have been disappointed to know my father was nothing even close to being the redneck he portrayed. He never hunted, cared little about NASCAR or pro wrestling and spent 90 percent of his free time reading. Some of the crazies, though, believed my old man to be a living, breathing comic-book character come to life. And none more so than Nasty Man.

Nasty Man was, well, nasty. To this day I don't know where he was from, even though he came to the station fifteen or twenty times during the four years Jimmy was in office. A cloud of blue smoke pouring from his vehicle always announced his arrival. He drove an old station wagon that was actually pieced together from several different models. It was dented, and the five or six different colors it was painted were scabbed over with rust. The car would have stood out anywhere, but Nasty Man wanted to make sure, I guess. The rear windows and both side panels were plastered with hundreds of the most obscene bumper stickers I'd ever read. It was an insult on wheels, and how he made it across state lines I'll never know. But the car had nothing on Nasty Man himself. This guy gave rude, crude and loud behavior a bad name. And sometimes I'm not even sure the man was crazy at all. Maybe he was some performance artist out to test the limits of politeness and hospitality. Whatever the case, the guy tried his damnedest to assault and abuse the senses of everybody within earshot and eyeshot. My first encounter with him was one day when he bounded into the station and roared out, "Whar's Billy?" Standing in the door was a big man in overalls and no shirt. He had about three days worth of beard on his face and his hair was as greasy as hell. And he was dirty. Everybody in town was used to dirt, being in a farming community and all, and nobody was afraid of getting a little earth under their fingernails. But Nasty Man was unwashed and filthy. Even his teeth were crusty and green. He took over the room, talking loud and slapping people on the back and spewing out horrible, sexual jokes. The regulars, who made sport of everybody, were strangely quiet, as if they could somehow feel this guy's madness and wanted no part of it. It didn't bother Nasty Man, though, not to be accepted right away. He acted as though he'd been born and raised in town and was familiar with everyone. Then he reached into his pockets and began withdrawing an amazing collection of, uh . . . sexual devices and dropping them on the bar. Devices of rubber and plastic, devices with tiny motors or cranks, devices near life-sized and some well beyond human proportions. When he'd emptied his pockets, he went out to his car and brought in more, laughing and babbling the

whole time. He scared us. After drinking a few beers and waiting for the old man to show up—thankfully, he never did—
Nasty Man gathered his toys and left. There was an audible
sigh of relief when he pulled out of the parking lot.
Unfortunately, he kept coming back. Sometimes in another
car. Sometimes with a woman who sat outside the station and
waited for him. But he always had his toys.

We were lucky, the whole town was, not to have had any
really bad experiences from all the attention. Most everybody
who came to Plains was on their best behavior. A few were
obnoxious, as could be expected with the number of people
passing through each day, but few left any kind of impression.

At home, it wasn't unusual at all to have strangers banging
on the door several times a day. Anyone could come into town
and within a matter of minutes find out where the old man
lived. Most wanted a picture with him and seemed surprised
to find he was at work. And the phone rang constantly. People
from all over the country wanted to talk to my dad. I don't
think anyone thought about changing the phone number and
it was in the book, on one of the two pages containing the
Plains listings. My sisters and I learned very quickly to find
out who was calling before passing the phone to my father. It
might have been one of his buddies, whom he always talked
to, or some guy from North Dakota who wanted the old man
to ask Jimmy about veteran's benefits. Every day brought
something new and unusual.

The one thing I'm most questioned about when someone dis-
covers my connection to the family is what it was like to have an
uncle who was president. And they seem disappointed almost to
find out how far removed from the situation my immediate family was. We were in the midst of things in Plains, but beyond its
borders, being a nephew didn't mean much. I've made friends of
people I probably never would have met. And I've learned some

things about politics, *real* politics, that I wish I never knew. But as far as a lot of perks and pluses, there were none. As a matter of fact, it's been more of a pain in the ass than most would imagine. Just being related sometimes drew the wrath of those who disagreed with what Jimmy was doing in office. I got screamed at in school by a girl whose brother died in Vietnam. She was in tears and a crowd had gathered. This was the day after Jimmy pardoned those who fled the country to avoid the war. I didn't, and still don't, know how to respond. Sometimes people would make remarks designed to provoke, but I quickly learned to keep my head down. And some people still insist on believing I get some kind of check each month from the government just because I'm Jimmy's nephew. And I've given up trying to convince some of them that I didn't grow up in a mansion being followed around by white-gloved servants bearing silver trays. More than once I've been accused of getting jobs just because of who my family is. It doesn't matter that it was months, and in one case a year, after I was hired that it was discovered. I don't think it will ever end, though. I finally accepted this ten years after Jimmy left office and I got a job working for the sanitation department in a small Tennessee town. There are still those who are convinced I used my family connections to secure that coveted position on the garbage truck.

The real excitement came in the form of the Inauguration. All of us received an invitation package with passes to parties and, most importantly, to the stage where Jimmy was to be sworn in. And sometimes it is still hard for me to believe I was there. It wasn't until years later that I understood the gravity of the whole thing.

Going to Washington, D.C., was a big deal for my sisters and me. Hell, it was a big deal for everybody. My mother insisted I get a suit for the swearing-in and I complied. It was your standard navy blue suit with a vest. But for the parties I wanted to be stylish and wear a tuxedo. A tuxedo *I* picked out. A tuxedo any sixteen-year-old boy living in South Georgia in the mid-1970s would be proud to wear. It was powder blue with a paisley cummerbund. The shirt was ruffled and the collar and cuffs were piped in blue. The bow tie was blue and the shoes a gleaming black, as if they'd just been dipped in a pail of varnish. Damn . . . I was cool.

The old man and a group of his friends chartered a commercial airliner. The party that January began at thirty thousand feet over the Eastern United States and didn't end for almost a week. Again, like the night of the election, I only remember snatches, bits and pieces, of the whole thing. We stayed at the Washington Hilton and the family had an entire floor. I went wild; drunk most of the time, half from the exhilaration of being there and half from the beer and liquor I easily snagged from in front of all the distracted adults. Occasionally, the old man and I would pass in the hall; me pretending to be sober and him all red-faced and grinning and squinty-eyed from alcohol. I doubt he remembered any more than I did. Stories are told from time to time about our visit to Washington and only then can I recall moments. I need others to help my memory. Depending on how you look at it, we either showed the Hilton what partying was all about or made complete asses of ourselves. There was a time when I could puff up and entrance a crowd with my version of how the Georgia boys came to town and, by God, showed 'em all in Washington how *we* did things. These days I look back, as much as I'm able, and cringe. Mama and my sisters bore my dad and me with the good graces they all still possess. How, I don't know. Why is an even greater mystery.

The day of the swearing-in was colder than hell and filled with a lot of rushing around. I remember walking down a street somewhere with my family and people calling out my father's name. He stopped and talked and signed autographs. I don't think I'd realized until that day that the old man had become a celebrity. And I don't know if I really liked it. In Plains, at least, it seemed as if it all could be somehow contained. That day, on the streets of Washington, D.C., I felt as though I was witness to the beginning of a new life for him. It became real.

We made it to the Capitol and took our seats on the huge podium along with our cousins and aunts and uncles. There were dignitaries and cabinet members and celebrities. We waited and gawked and waited some more. And then Jimmy was sworn in and he gave his speech. My sister Jana and I sat together. In front of us was Shirley Temple Black, and Jana was starstruck. She ached to reach out and touch the lady's fur hat. We spent the whole time discussing whether she should or not, and in the process we missed most of being witness to history.

And then we went to the White House; my first and only visit. We didn't stay long—just enough to become goggle-eyed at our surroundings. I have pictures to remind me of the time. My mother visited on several occasions and my father many more. But it was only that once for my sisters and me.

There was any number of parties to choose from that night. We had passes to several but my sisters and I went to only one, the Georgia Ball. The crowd was too large for anyone to do anything but stand around and listen to the band, and beer at the cash bar was six dollars a six-pack. *Six dollars!* I was too young to buy any but, inconspicuous in my blue tuxedo, I crept around the fringes and waited for the right moment. Some wealthy guy came up and bought five six-packs. To reach his wallet he had to put them on the floor beside his feet, and I zoomed in and snatched two of them while he was occupied with paying the bartender. I was drunk before we left for the Hilton.

The sixth floor was a free-for-all. Every room was open and people overflowed out into the hallway. I wandered in and out and up and down, just as cool as hell in my rented threads, helping myself to the free beer and booze. I had reached the point of having to close one eye to see straight when someone grabbed me by the back of my collar and spun me around. For a few minutes, the crowd around me was vastly entertained by the sight of Mama wagging her finger in my face and giving me hell. She pulled me into one of the rooms and made me go to bed. Even the protection of the powder blue tuxedo couldn't save me.

I think all of us were ready to go home by the time we left. Washington was as far removed from my town as any place I'd ever been and, in truth, it scared me a little bit. Plains looked good from where I was. There'd been enough adventure, a whole year of it, and it was time to go home and exhale and get back to being normal.

Right.

Chapter Thirteen

I don't have many things to remind me of my old man during the mid to late seventies. There is an empty Billy Beer can on the shelf above me. Beside it is the Coke can commemorating the 1991 Braves for being the National League champs. I think I would trade the one with my father's name on it before I would part with the can lauding the Braves. The few pictures I have of him when he was "Billy Carter" are hidden away in an old walnut box. Years pass between the times the light of day falls on them. The one I do keep visible is an eight-by-ten black-and-white of what used to be a typical day at the station. There are no strangers out front, only the old man and me and a few of the regulars. The building itself wears its shabbiness and the crooked signs and the oil spots on the concrete pad like a comfortable old coat, and there is a straw broom propped against the drink machine. It's as if all the bullshit that had been piled upon the town was somehow swept away for a brief moment and the old Plains beneath it was revealed. I know it was taken by a man who had no reason to be there other than that Jimmy and Plains were in the news. But that's all right. I can't see him.

The one other item I keep out in the open is a box containing a plastic model issued by Revell. I've never attempted to put it together so it is still in pieces. It's not the model itself I keep around but rather the box. It makes me laugh. BILLY CARTER'S "REDNECK POWER PICK-UP" the box proclaims. Below that is a picture of my old man grinning through the window of a chromed-up and decal-ed white Chevy pick-up with wooden bed rails. The look on his face is one of a person who is curiously unattached to what is going on in the moment. A look, to me at least, of resignation. And there is the glow of the drinker about him. A glow we all had become increasingly familiar with by the time that picture was taken. But I don't dwell on the photo. I don't find it funny and my eyes slide over the face. What makes me laugh is the description on the side of the box. "A one-of-a-kind pick-up for a one-of-a-kind guy!" the box says. "Whether he's on service runs or just running around town, he does it in style with his REDNECK POWER PICK-UP!" And it goes on about what a good ol' boy, redneck my father was. The truck was real, lent to my father by Revell as a promotional deal. I don't know where it is now but I'm glad it's gone. What's funny to me about all of this is how quickly he was labeled with the image and how easily everyone gobbled it up. I don't think my old man ever made a "service run." He barely knew one end of a screwdriver from the other. And the "redneck" thing began as a joke played on the press. They didn't know where else to put him, and the joke grew and grew and grew until it became much bigger than the real Billy Carter.

So I guess the reason my home is not a museum to that time, why my walls are not covered with pictures and clippings and T-shirts and such, is because I know none of it was true. Oh, it all happened. And my old man, by choice,

participated; making the appearances and giving the interviews and basically selling himself from one end of the
country to the other. But for me to remember those years as
somehow being his glory days does a great disservice to my
father. It gives more power to those three or four years when
he seemed to stumble around, sometimes in desperation,
than they deserve. I know most pictures taken of him in
those few years show only the animated shell of the man; a
man who was once a thousand times more alive.

To say that none of us, my family, was excited about the old
man's notoriety would be a lie. In the beginning, being known
as Billy Carter's son or daughter was a pretty damn good
thing. The tourists' attention was fun for a while and the little bit of interest we got from the press was flattering. And
the old man was the perfect contrast to Jimmy. His beer-
drinking, shoot-from-the-hip, not-give-a-damn attitude
played like a dream off of Jimmy's I'll-never-lie-to-you,
Sunday-school-teacher demeanor. A better pairing couldn't
have been planned. But what most people don't realize is that
my dad was treating all the fuss as a diversion, a hobby of
sorts. It was an excuse to party and to have fun at the expense
of the press and the tourists. That people were willing to pay
him to do TV shows and appear at mall openings just made
it all that much more fun. He knew it was a joke and I think
a lot of the press who came around in that first year knew it,
too. They needed diversions and the old man was willing and
affable as hell, if they caught him in the right place at the
right time. He was always good for a story or a borderline
unprintable quote. But that was all good times, all for fun.
Whatever role he played as the good ol' boy, redneck brother
was just that—a role. His job as manager of the family business came first. And he still took that job seriously.

There was a time in the farming business when there were no

government policies to abide by or hundred-thousand-dollar combines. A farmer had land that was more than likely passed down to him from his father. Land that was first plowed and planted by his grandfather or great-grandfather. And that farmer knew every tree and every inch of his acreage better than any office worker knows the corners of his eight-by-eight cubicle. He had his seed and his tractor and his plow. Most importantly, he had his family. And each and every member in turn grew to know the land as well as all those before. They knew the hard work and the responsibility. To call farming a profession or a job or a career somehow belittles the people who are born to it. It is something you live. There are no yearly raises, no pension plans, no vacations or time off. And, thankfully, there are no committee meetings or feasibility studies or colored charts and graphs to worry about. But there is the weather. And, as of yet, there is no board of pale and pasty men in striped ties gathered around a shiny conference table delegating rain. I'm sure they are trying, though, and I fear it is coming.

But until then, it is the farmer and his family who face the good years and the bad years together. They are the ones who wake every morning to ride their land and hope the magic has flowed in overnight and turned the plowed red dirt into a carpet of soft green. They are the ones who worry that the beauty of a clear blue sky portends weeks of dry ground. A late frost blanketing two-inch shoots means plowing under and replanting; it means gallons more of sweat. And still these people don't walk away. All that God gives them, good or bad, they accept as part of the cycle. And sometimes "Just wait 'til next year" is a real prayer for the farmer. Sometimes, next year is all he has.

My father and my mother understood this. They knew the people they did business with were much, much more than inked numbers in a ledger. They knew those columns of credits and debits represented lives. A written figure could sometimes mean the difference between a farmer being able to afford to plant 100 acres or 150 acres. It could mean the farmer's child might have to come home for a while before finishing college or that the old Ford tractor will *have* to somehow make it through one more season. My folks understood "Just wait 'til next year" and that next year always comes. Not always on time, but it comes.

My father formed his connection to the land and the farmers from the first time he followed his daddy through the fields. That connection only grew stronger as he aged. There were times in his life when he went away but was always drawn back by the tug of the land. And when he was finally given the job of running the warehouse, he slipped into the position as if it had been waiting for him always. He felt he was where he rightfully ought to be. The days of rising at 4 A.M. to ride the roads and look at the land were in no way a burden to him. The late nights at the dryers and the hectic days of peanut season were like new blood thrumming through his veins. How much he cared for the farmers was evident in the way they dealt with him. They knew he was made of the same things as they were. He was one of them. During the time the old man ran the warehouse, he *was* the business. There was no way to think of one without the other coming to mind. And the place thrived.

Jimmy owned a majority of the family business. When he became president, all of his interests had to be placed in blind trust. This included control of the warehouse. Whether this was known to my father before Jimmy was elected, I don't know. I don't recall the old man being concerned about the matter. If he was, as usual, he kept it to himself. I am sure, though, it never crossed his mind to think someone would question his ability to manage the one thing he'd spent his life

around. But the questions soon began to trickle down to my
father from Atlanta. Questions as to why certain farmers were
behind a few months on their accounts; questions about the
day-to-day running of the business. At first the phone calls
and the correspondences were no more than minor annoy-
ances, and Atlanta was too far away to worry about.

It is easy for me, still, to think of those trying to run the
warehouse from 130 miles away as "Them." I never met any of
the people, wouldn't know Them now if they walked into the
room. And I *like* to imagine Them as a group of faceless men
wearing suits and ties, gathered around a mile-long conference
table in a carpeted room atop the tallest building in the city. The
room is thermostatically controlled, safe, and sealed against the
elements. I imagine the sun shines harmlessly through filtered,
floor-to-ceiling windows and there is an invisible hint, just a
hint, of muted fragrances from bottled colognes floating
through the air. Papers glide endlessly back and forth across the
polished top of the table, shuffled by manicured hands. I don't
imagine much talking, though, only lawyerly shakes of the head
or a raised eyebrow or two. God forbid the dignified silence be
broken by an expressed opinion. It is too easy not to question
the ink on the pages before them. It is better not to think that
those 8½-by-11 pieces of paper represent real people. Real people would have real problems beyond the columns of black or
red and could not be filed away and forgotten when five o'clock
rolled around. It is easier to believe not much exists outside the
filtered windows or beneath the room atop that tallest building.
I like to imagine that those men would be lost away from the
interstates or the shadows of skyscrapers. And it makes me
smile to think of them sweating through their suits in the middle of an eighty-acre field, dust-covered, and fearful that their
country club of a world has vanished, leaving them to make a
living with their hands.

I *have* to imagine these things. It makes me feel better about the way things happened. To accept that those handling Jimmy's interests were only doing the job they were given leaves me with no one to rave against; it waves in my face that my anger has been wasted. To find there were no diabolical plans to undermine my father and take from him the one thing that kept his life in line somehow makes the situation worse. It's as if he didn't matter and that he could simply be brushed aside with a wave of one of those tender, manicured hands.

Farmers, who for years had done business with my family, came to my father and asked about the changes. Some couldn't understand why decisions concerning their lives were being made in Atlanta by people they didn't know, and so they took their business elsewhere. Many of them, before leaving, talked to my father about it first and told him they would stay if *he* wanted them to. They trusted him and knew they could count on him to give them the advice they needed. The problem was that he was as much in the dark about what was going on as the farmers were, and he told them so. He told them he didn't want them to leave but he couldn't honestly tell them what was going to happen. And he couldn't blame anyone, he said, for wanting to take their business to those who understood and respected them.

I do know any attempts my father made to express his concerns to those in charge were ignored. And when he obtained the backing and the money to buy control of the business, the offer wasn't even considered. No one knows why. But it *is* agreed, by farmers and friends and most family members alike, that if the old man had been given the opportunity to continue running the business the way he had been, without the Atlanta influence, the warehouse would still be in the family. And it is a fact that Carter's Warehouse started losing money only after the business was placed in blind trust. A lot of money. The last year my father was in control, we processed about twenty-five thousand tons of peanuts. The year the lawyers took over only about fifteen hundred tons were bought. The math is easy.

It is still a mystery as to why my father was ignored the way he was. I know he didn't meekly stand aside and whine. He raised hell. Close friends lobbied those in control on his behalf, but no one listened. And no one knows why. It seems to me that anyone claiming proficiency in business matters would have been hesitant to meddle; they would have been content just to guide a bit and watch the business grow. But it was as if the plan was to slash and burn and stumble and fall.

I realize that when the warehouse was placed in blind trust those in control had no obligation whatsoever to confer with my father on anything. He was once again just a hired hand in a business he thought of as his own. But there were some instances seemingly designed as blatant slaps in his face. It is hard to look at them as anything but. My mother and my father had taken a trip to Florida to get away for a few days. Both of them needed it—the old man for the stress and frustration he'd been dealing with because of the warehouse, and my mother for having to deal with him through all of it. I remember standing in the office, looking out a window, when three or four large trucks, one with a crane, pulled up. They stopped and a man came in and asked where the cotton gin was. They were there to dismantle it, he said. It had been sold. No one in the office had heard about it. My folks were tracked down and hours later they returned to Plains. The old man was livid at not being told of this major decision. I think it was then he decided to leave.

They say there are no mistakes made in the offices atop the tallest buildings, only bad business decisions. And not once, ever, have I expected anyone to admit to a big-time, royal fuckup. It's as if you're born with the knowledge that those in control are incapable of claiming errors as their own. They *can't* be wrong. They *can't* be flawed.

There was a feeble gesture made to get my father to stay on. He told them he'd rather fry in Hell. And I think he truly would have rather than be party to what he saw as the destruction of his daddy's business.

My father's leaving was like the last breath pulled from a body; like the light in an eye growing dim.

The family business died.

Chapter Fourteen

I've wondered a lot how the ending of that one chapter in my old man's life was handled around the conference table in Atlanta. Was it with a shrug and the closing of a folder and then the directive to move on to other matters? I hope not. I would like to think someone leaned back in a leather chair and maybe gave a moment to questioning themselves about how things were handled. But I know it didn't happen. The ones I think of as Them are not the types to challenge their own abilities.

It has been written on more than one occasion that when Jimmy came back from Washington after his term as president, he was broke and found the family business in ruins. Carter's Warehouse was more than a million dollars in debt. This is all true. It has also been written that my father managed the business the four years Jimmy was away. This is not true. My father left barely a year after Jimmy took office. The warehouse began to lose money only after he was gone. Whoever was in control for the next three years is the one responsible for the end of the business built by my grandfather's hands, not my father.

The old man was not the type to chase after something after he had let it go. It was years before he set foot on warehouse property again, and then only for a visit. By that time the business was under another name, run by a corporation. The family feel was gone. It always bothered me that he never felt the need to take up for himself concerning the matter of the warehouse. He allowed the implications that he led the business to failure to go unchallenged. But he lost the battle fought with the big dogs and knew, even then, that the victors write the histories. And, too, by the time those four years were over, any protests my father made about anything were met with slight smiles and raised eyebrows and a "Well . . . it's Billy. What do you expect?"

It was a shock not to have the warehouse in our lives anymore. This shock was doubled by my family packing up and leaving Plains. The decision was made to move after waking one morning to find a tour bus parked in our yard and people peering through our windows with cameras. They were all offended when they were asked to leave and huffed away muttering about how rude we were. We moved twenty miles away, six miles from Buena Vista, Georgia, and the big old house on Bond Street stood empty of anything but the invisible bits and pieces of ourselves we all left behind. I don't remember if I looked back.

The business and our home in Plains, the roots, were gone, hacked away, and my father's slow death began.

It wasn't evident at first. Hell, things were good. The old man was a full-fledged celebrity by this time and it seemed everybody wanted him. He appeared on *Hee Haw* several times and the Merv Griffin show. He signed on with an agent out of Nashville and began to travel constantly, bringing in five to ten thousand dollars a day. All the talk shows wanted him: *Donahue, Tom Snyder*, etc. He drove the pace car at the

Daytona 500 one year and appeared at uncountable mall openings and conventions. The only thing expected of him was to be Billy Carter and to drink beer and say things others were hesitant to say, and he handled himself in fine form. His honesty made him a folk hero, a cult figure, and I think he was as amazed by his popularity as all the rest of us were.

The money poured in and poured out just as quickly. Our new house in Buena Vista was damn-near a mansion sitting on eighty acres of land. The first thing the old man did was have another wing built, adding a big den and three more bedrooms. There was a swimming pool. It was a beautiful place but it never really became home. The old man bought a 1976 Cadillac El Dorado, black, with a burgundy leather interior and gangster whitewalls. It was one hell of a car. All of us kids of driving age had our own vehicles. None of us wanted for anything. Some of the parties the old man hosted are still talked about to this day. No one could ever fault him for not being generous. And everybody had fun. Too much, sometimes.

Just being on the fringes of fame does weird things to some people. You begin to think you're dusted with glitter or gold and that being born into a certain family is somehow an accomplishment. You develop a strut; an attitude that I imagine is quite sickening to watch. It happened to me. I allowed it. My age at the time had something to do with it, but not a lot. It was almost as if the hidden parts of my personality, the one's kept under control by the manners I was taught, by the way I was raised, somehow forced themselves to the surface. And I thought it was okay. Hell, my old man was famous; I could do what I wanted, act the way I felt like acting. I really believed I was special; I was touched by the great god of good fortune. The special treatment I was getting was something I never questioned. As far as I was concerned, I deserved it. And all for just being in the shadow of someone who was in the shadow of someone else. It all went to the head. I became that most awful of awful people: the teenaged asshole. And I was only brushed by the light. Just a touch. The old man got it full force.

The warehouse was out of the picture and the only job my father had was being Billy Carter. He still had the station and was there whenever he wasn't on the road. Most of his other time was spent at a big, round table in the restaurant at the Best Western motel in Americus, holding court with his buddies.

Plains had become a bona fide, twenty-four-hour-a-day, seven-day-a-week sideshow. Tourists paid money to board a van and take a fifteen-minute tour of the town. Every day there were protesters picketing on the sidewalk, waving signs, hoping to get in the news. The only ones who had any impact at all were the farmers, who came to Plains from all over the country, rallying for 100 percent parity. They brought their tractors with them, hundreds and hundreds, and blocked Highway 280 for more than a day, then camped out in the park overnight. The station averaged at least one bomb threat a week. Five minutes before the supposed blast was to take place, all the regulars would take their beers and walk across the street and watch. Two or three minutes after deadline, they'd walk back across and reclaim their seats. The old water tower in the center of town was cut into pieces and hauled away. A new one was built just at the edge of town. All three major networks moved mobile homes around the base of it and the area became known as TV City. More crazy people came. Some stayed for a while. A famous model came to town and did a photo shoot surrounded by quaint Southern people and standing in the doorways of cute little shacks. Plains Baptist Church made the news for not allowing a black man to attend services and the congregation split. The Plains Police Department grew from one part-time officer to three full-time. A giant Styrofoam peanut, complete with a wide, big-toothed grin, appeared out in front of the local convenience store. Mr. Joe's place, the beer joint a few miles outside of town, was renamed the Plains Country Club. Though the name was changed, the atmosphere remained the same. Many a tourist got no further than the screen door before fleeing. The city council decided the community Christmas tree, a cut cedar erected and then strung with lights by the citizens, was no longer worthy of our town. City money was spent on a hideous, plastic thing the color of a garbage bag adorned with orange spheres the size of beach balls. It disappeared one night down 280, throwing a shower of sparks from its metal ribs, roped behind a speeding pick-up truck. The old man was questioned by the Georgia Bureau of Investigation about the tree kidnapping. He'd been vocal about abandoning the tradition. But he was in New York at the time the tree was taken and the G.B.I. still doesn't know what happened. It's amazing what a phone call and the promise of a case of beer can accomplish. Town folks grew to know national media personalities on a first-name basis. The old man took a liking to leisure suits and cowboy boots and soon had a closet full of each. The town was transformed into a county fair. One that wouldn't pack its shit after a week and go away. The only ones not affected, it seemed, were the older citizens, who'd already seen everything from great depressions to world wars, and the farmers, who had no time for such silliness.

And just like the town, my father changed; becoming a skewed version of himself. The one thing that'd kept structure to his life, the one thing he'd thought of as always being there, was gone. To see the warehouse, his father's business, put in the hands of someone he knew didn't care for it as much as he did hurt him. To find out there were those who didn't have faith enough in him to allow him to continue running the warehouse after he'd proven, time and again, he was born to the job, hurt him even more. It was a hard kick in the ass. After that, I don't think he cared anymore.

Sometimes I blame the change in my father on anybody but him. I blame the press. I blame Jimmy. I blame all the people who asked for his autograph and the people who took pictures of him. Sometimes I blame everybody in the world. It makes it easier than to have to accept that he brought everything on himself. But always, after soothing myself with false finger-pointing on his behalf, I settle down and face what was. Maybe things would have been better for everybody if my father had stuck it out at the warehouse. Maybe if we'd all ignored everything going on around us and pretended our lives were still normal we could have continued on as before. Maybe.

But one thing had always been certain. Even though the old man had stepped cleanly and neatly into his place in life, that as manager of the family business, his personality never changed. There was always that Carter temper. Granted, it didn't surface as much when he controlled the warehouse, but it was still there. He would put his fist through windows on occasion when things didn't go his way. The quick, cold stare was still a favorite weapon; a split-second warning that he was about to erupt. But for the most part he kept himself calm and never allowed that temper to interfere with his running of the business. When he realized his opinion didn't matter anymore, though, when he finally understood the lawyer in Atlanta, and a lot of other people for that matter, would forever think of him as the baby brother, that temper took control. He was quick to declare himself finished with the business. Whether it was just to prove a point, I'll never know. No one will. Though I wanted to, I never asked my father about those days. I never asked him if he wished he could go back a few years and do things differently. I wanted to ask him if he thought it would have been better just to hold on tightly and wait for the storm to pass; to put up with the bullshit for a while. But I didn't. By the time I'd grown up enough to wonder about those things and just maybe had the courage to question, my father was tired of it all and damn-near a beaten man. To ask at all, I think, would have been too much like doubting him. And, God knows, he'd been doubted enough.

There were times in my life when I thought I had my father pegged. And, of course, as soon as that happened he'd do something to change my perception and the whole discovery process would have to start all over again. My mother, who knew him better than anyone, even had difficulty sometimes finding the words to explain him.

I do know that the year and a half after he left the warehouse was close to being the worst time of his life. It wouldn't seem so. There were parties and money and everywhere he went he was treated royally. But he'd developed a "fuck it all" attitude and climbed full-time into the "Billy Carter" character. Except this time that character was not always the genial, good ol' boy people had grown to expect. His words became sharper at times, meaner, with seemingly little regard for their effect on himself or the rest of the family. Stories about him spotlighted his drinking; his inability to recognize when he'd gone too far with the things he said. His disease took over and that little voice in the back of his head that had once been dulled to a whisper fully woke and became a full-fledged roar. And it gibbered and cavorted and played and told the old man he could do whatever the hell he wanted to do. And he listened.

The strange and wonderful times were close to being over. The magic in the air, the feeling that all things good were ours if only we wanted them, was replaced by a dull ache, a queasiness, in the pit of the stomach.

The old man began to fall fast. And hard.

Chapter Fifteen

For years after my father died I made excuses to myself, and to anyone else who would listen, about his drinking. "What would you do," I'd ask, "if someone came to you and said they were going to fly you out to California for a week, put you up in the best hotel, treat you like a celebrity and pay you five or six thousand dollars a day? And, oh yeah, drink all you want to. As a matter of fact, we *want* you to drink. That's what you do, isn't it . . . drink and say funny shit?" The standard response most times was for people to look at me as if I was crazier than hell for even asking such a question. The majority agreed they would make the trip, take the check, then drink themselves into a blind, running drunk. Most people, though, after maybe one hard night, would slow down and take a rest and allow the pounding in their head to remind them that their body wasn't made for such abuse. The old man, on the other hand, was not like most others. When that voice in his head finally cranked up the volume and he *chose* to listen to it, when he decided he had nothing left to lose, he began to drink in earnest. All those years of recreational drinking just served as a warm-up.

Playtime was over. He used to say he was in search of the perfect buzz, and damned if he didn't spend most of every waking moment trying to find it.

For a long time it was easy to claim my father would have
never reached that point with his drinking if not for becoming a celebrity. But there is no doubt he would've. It's only a
matter of time with any alcoholic before life goes out of control. I do think the process sped up for my father, though,
with his years in the spotlight. Hell, as far as he was concerned there was no reason *not* to drink. For a while he was
the ambassador for good times. On the front of his business
card was the spent tab from a beer can. Beneath it was simply "Billy Carter." This was the late '70s, during the CB
craze, and the old man's handle was "Cast Iron." He got the
name when someone, amazed at his ability to drink and drink
and drink, claimed the old man's stomach must be made of
cast iron. You couldn't find a story printed about him that
didn't mention the ever-present drink in his hand. And I
think the old man tried hard to live up to the image he'd created. But he did have the press pegged. Reverend Earl
Dukes, a good friend of our family, told my father one time
he hoped he wasn't drinking as much as the papers claimed.
"Brother Earl," my father replied, "there's no way in *hell* I can
drink as much as they say I do."

I sure wasn't complaining about the old man's attitude
towards drinking. Any chance for me to grab a bottle or two
of Blue Nun wine from the cases beneath the carport was
always taken. And I started drinking openly in front of him
when I was seventeen. The night I graduated from high
school, he provided a keg of beer and a case of champagne for
my friends and me. As I said before, there was not a thing in
world wrong, as a teenager, with having one of the best-
known beer drinkers of all time for a father. It was good for

my social standing, and I tried damned hard to follow in his footsteps. To drink with the old man, though, was to drink with the big dogs, and I didn't stand a chance.

There were still some good times going on during this period. Though my father drank most of the time, he still kept up pretty well with what was going on around him. He was contracted time and again for promotions and events by some of the same groups, groups that had worked with every celebrity in the book, because, in their words, of how easy he was to deal with. And he'd do anything for charity. From getting into the ring with Joe Frasier for a mock fight to taking hot-air-balloon rides, even though he was terrified of heights. And some of the best friends my father ever had were made while he was on the road. Friends who remained friends even when the old man became an untouchable of sorts. He appeared in a made-for-TV movie, "Flatbed Annie and Sweetie Pie—Lady Truckers," which proved, beyond a doubt, that the old man was at his best left without a script. When Jimmy came home for visits, my dad always challenged him to a softball game. Jimmy pitched for his team, which consisted of off-duty Secret Service agents. It was rumored that a ringer or two was always brought in, as if already having some of the best-conditioned federal agents in the country weren't enough. They played seriously to win against the old man as pitcher and his team of reporters and technicians and whoever else didn't mind being humiliated in front of several hundred tourists. My dad's team usually began the game a few hours before first pitch down at the station for a pep rally and many, many beers. The pep rally continued during the game and most times ended well into the night, long after they'd, once again, been beaten all to hell by my uncle's team. But whatever the occasion, TV or radio show, rodeo, convention appearance or softball game, if my father was there, so was alcohol.

So it didn't surprise anyone when the old man was approached by Falls City Brewing Company, out of Louisville, Kentucky, to use his name on a brand of beer. And Billy Beer was born. It was distributed in one of the, I think, most attractive cans on the market. The can was orange and white with my father's name in blue. At the top, above the name, in tiny letters, it said: "Brewed expressly for and with the personal approval of one of America's all-time great beer drinkers—Billy Carter." Below the name was a quote from the old man: "I had this beer brewed up just for me. I think it's the best I ever tasted. And I've tasted a lot. I think you'll like it, too." The only problem was, the old man readily admitted a few years later, he was drunk when he chose from the four different brews submitted to him. The beer picked to bear his name was pretty much a casual decision. Some argue that it was a fine beer. I am not one of those. Billy Beer was strong and heavy and a couple could kick my young ass all over town. The only time I remember drinking more than one was on Billy Beer Day, when they had the unveiling in Plains. It was October 31, 1978, Halloween. There was a Billy Beer hot-air balloon behind the station and a couple of Billy Beer beer trucks. The trucks were packed with case upon case, and cans were sold at a one-time-only price of five cents each. Of course, I got it for free. And found myself ending Billy Beer Day in Lebanon Cemetery, howling at the moon. The old man was careful thereafter to be seen drinking only Billy Beer. When he was among friends, though, or there were no cameras around, he was loyal to Pabst Blue Ribbon.

There came a time when beer wasn't enough. My father had always been known to drink liquor on occasion, but as far as I know, it wasn't his drink of choice. But soon all of his real drinking involved vodka. He got to a point where he said he only drank beer to sober up. I don't know how much he actually drank every day. I've heard stories about him killing a fifth at a sitting, then getting up for more. I *have* seen him put away more than one half-pint in an hour's time. As far as the number of beers he could drink in a day, well, they were damn-near uncountable, and there weren't many of his buddies who could hang with him when he decided to get serious. And in the last of his drinking days, he actually clinked when he walked from all the vodka miniatures and half-pints he had stuffed in his pockets and even in his boots. Whatever way you look at it, good or bad, when it came to drinking, the old man was a world-class contender.

I feel like an idiot sometimes when I think back on how long it took me to recognize that my father was an alcoholic. One time I was on the road with him and I witnessed him drink a half-pint of vodka the moment he woke up, before even putting his feet on the floor, yet I didn't think anything of it. Why should I? As long as I'd been alive, my father had been drinking. All of us had grown up watching him walk through the door a couple of times a week with that flush-faced glow about him. We learned early on to let him be when he was in one of his "moods." And I don't think any of us, my sisters and I, at that time had yet learned of my father's flirtation with Alcoholics Anonymous so many years before.

But something was happening and it wasn't good. The one or two day trips away from home became five or six days with only a day in between before he left again. It was all in the name of providing for the family and I'm sure it was, with him having no other way to make a living. But he liked it, too. He liked it a lot. On the road there were no rules; no one to lay an eye upon him the way only my mother could. Though my father was the undisputed king of our family, he still knew better than to raise the wrath of Sybil. More and more, his expected dates of return would be put off a day, sometimes two. And he would either come home repentant as hell (every once in a while) or in a foul, black humor, pissed at the world and at all of us in particular (more often than not). Most times at home, he shut down completely; became unapproachable and had little to say to anyone. It was as if he had given everything to strangers and had little left for us. The brittle times were back and all of us walked and talked very carefully, afraid that even our everyday activities would somehow set him off. And even though there came a time when we began to dread his return from the road, when we were almost as eager for him to leave again as he was, we couldn't help wanting to be around him. That spark remained, the one that made him our dad, the one that called all the attention to him in the first place. Whatever it was, he had it until the day he died.

A good friend of my father's, one of his best, told me once to remember that everything, *everything*, my father did during those times, good or bad, was done under the influence of alcohol. That even on the rare days he didn't drink, he still couldn't separate himself from his disease. Don't ever forget that, my father's friend said, and think kindly on him when you remember those days . . . think kindly on him.

But I heard those words only after my father was dead. Whether they could have changed the way I began to feel about him during the last years of the seventies, I don't know. I would like to remember myself as being big enough to easily forgive, but I wasn't.

It seemed he was trying hard to become an embarrassment, to mortify me and the rest of my family. The things he began to say and do in public were seemingly done for shock value or to create controversy. Outright laughter at his earlier antics became nervous, and I was quick to change the subject when my dad was talked about. He wasn't funny anymore. To me, at least, to *me*, he was almost pathetic.

Oh, we all still defended him against the snide remarks and put-downs that popped up more and more often in the papers and magazines, but we knew some, maybe most, were deserved. He seemed to willingly stumble around the country placing himself in unflattering and controversial positions. He'd do anything under the influence of alcohol. I watched in mild horror once as he stood on the set of a national TV show and allowed the host to strap a jester's cap made from beer tabs on his head. My father was grinning as he stood there, all aglow from liquor, idly flipping the bell dangling from the hat. Another time he was photographed sitting on a throne made of cases of beer. I was embarrassed for him. No, I was embarrassed for myself. The chore came with opening the daily papers to see if he'd committed another cringing offense. If he hadn't, I could exhale for at least a while. If he had, I lowered my head a bit and plowed through the day. Other times I could only shake my head and wonder what in the hell he was thinking about. I remember once driving the twenty miles to Buena Vista from Americus, where I was attending Georgia Southwestern, with a load of clothes to wash. When I arrived home, there was a strange car parked out front. I entered and heard voices from the living room. Mama was in the kitchen, nervous and flustered. "What's wrong?" I asked. Before she answered, my father came in and said there was someone he wanted me to meet. In the living room were three men in suits. One was a little, short guy wearing glasses. The old man introduced him as the Imperial Wizard of one of the factions of the Ku Klux Klan. The man was polite to a fault and offered his hand, but I walked out as the old man stood glaring at me. The man hadn't been invited into our home because of any racist attitudes my father had, but because he was trying to prove a point—which was, he would do whatever the hell he felt like doing, regardless of who his brother was. I don't think I've ever seen my mother as mad as she was that day. The old man was adamant, though, by that time that no one was going to muzzle him or control his actions. And meeting with a Grand Whatever of the K.K.K. was just one of his ways of letting the world know. I think that was the moment when I began to become more than just an extension of my father. A little crack appeared and *I* peeked out. I had to choose between shaking the hand of a man I despised or raise the wrath of the old man. I took the hard way.

It wasn't long after that I realized just how much of a drinking problem my father had. I went to Oklahoma City with him and a couple of his buddies for a three-day event. A mall opening, I think. From the moment we left home, the old man was drinking. Drinking hard. It seemed whatever my father did that weekend was contrary to what the promoter desired. He fulfilled his contract, but not without constant headbutting with the guy in charge. It even reached the point where the promoter asked me to speak to my father and see if I could calm him a bit. I laughed.

My father was presented with a full, ceremonial headdress by a group of Native American Indians from the area and made an honorary tribe member. He behaved himself during the ceremony, sensing somehow the gravity of what was being bestowed. But those of us with him still held our breath. We all knew he was capable, damn-near guaranteed, in fact, of saying something only he found humorous; of making a statement someone would have to later explain away. He did good, though, and handled himself well for those couple of hours in that three-day weekend.

I was glad when the time came to leave. I felt as though I'd spent the whole trip babysitting. But I hadn't, really. I was just trying to stay out of the way. Mark Fuller, the man who'd been traveling with my dad pretty much from the beginning, was the official Billy Carter handler. He was the guy who put out fires and reassured the promoters. But the old man had reached such a point with his drinking that he wouldn't listen to anyone anymore. Mark was exhausted by trip's end and had accepted the fact my dad was finally beyond anyone's control.

Somehow we made it to the airport and take-off was uneventful. But as soon as the flight leveled off, the old man pulled that beautiful, floor-length headdress from the compartment and put it on. He sat in the aisle, wearing a ceremonial Indian headdress, black horn-rimmed glasses, and a green leisure suit. And he was drunk. Had been for three days. He folded his arms and began to chant. "Hi-yi-yi-yi. Hi-yi-yi-yi." Over and over. Funny? Not a bit. The stewardess, polite at first, kept asking him to return to his seat. When he didn't, after repeated requests, she threatened to get the captain. I was a few rows back, making myself small and hoping like hell no one made the connection between me and the guy embarrassing himself at thirty-thousand feet. I glanced around, noticing the looks of mild disgust on the faces of the other passengers. Mark sat silently. He'd given up. And I don't blame him.

The old man got out of the aisle finally, but only after the stewardess had chewed his ass like it had never been chewed before. That, at least, made it through the fog in his head. When we landed in Atlanta, all I was thinking about was that there was only a two-hour drive left of this trip and I could get away. As we walked down the concourse, I knew the man beside me, my father, was nothing more than a moving piece of meat. He was on automatic. People called out his name and asked for autographs and slapped his back and shook his hand. He responded to all of this with a vacant grin and a giggle. We reached the end of the concourse, having to turn right or left, and the old man kept moving forward. He stopped only when he met the wall, and stood there, with his face pressed to the wallpaper. I took his arm, while people watched, and guided him away. All I could think was, "This man is fucked-up."

My father wasn't funny anymore; he wasn't cute.

He was sick and he was sad and I began to hate him.

My trip to Oklahoma was one of the few eyewitness accounts, on my part, to my father's behavior. We rarely went with him to any of his appearances. Most of what we learned he was doing away from home we learned like everyone else, through the media. To be fair to him, I know now some of the things written were distorted and that there seemed to be a conscious effort by some in the press to look for things to put him down about. But, again, my father never laid the blame for anything he did on anyone but himself.

The week-long drunks, the fights, the inappropriate remarks, all the downright stupid shit he got involved in were hard on the family, to be sure. My mother especially. She waited at home for him while he was away all the time and took care of the family. If possible, she was more in the dark about what the old man was up to than anybody. But she was the one who comforted the rest of us; she made everything seem all right. She held us together. And that's remarkable, considering what was about to hit us next.

The old man's alcoholism and the effect it had on everyone was minor compared to what was around the corner.

What was lurking was a little episode those of us in the family refer to as the "Libya Thing."

Chapter Sixteen

The Libya Thing.

What the hell was that all about?

Well . . . I don't really know.

I don't feel too bad about it either, because the United States government spent close to 30 million in 1970s dollars trying to figure it out, and even they couldn't come up with an answer to satisfy anyone. The whole thing kind of faded away after the 1980 election. But while it was going on, the only true way it could be described was as a nightmare. An "Oh my God, what has the old man gotten himself into now?" nightmare.

Of course, I, just like everyone else in the family, wasn't privy to all the information concerning my dad's Libyan deal. As with everything else going on in his life, this, too, he kept mostly to himself. I do know the whole thing began while the old man was still drinking. And I can reasonably figure that the reason he was approached in the first place was because of who his brother was. I can also attest, beyond a doubt, that the effect the Libya Thing had on my mother, my sisters, my brother, and me, rivaled—even far surpassed—any stunt he'd pulled before. And though alcohol was the true culprit, the Libya Thing was probably the last push that ended with the old man hitting bottom. He learned very quickly there was a big difference between running the family peanut business and stepping up to bat in the world of international trade.

Ideally, the Libya Thing would have begun in a smoky bar down around the equator somewhere. There'd be slow-turning ceiling fans and palms and, over in the corner in a rattan chair, a fat man wearing a fez. All the players would be well dressed in either leather jackets or linen suits and every spoken word would be a work of art. And then the obvious villain would appear, sidling through the door. He'd approach the hero, who sat coolly at the brass-railed, mahogany bar staring pensively into the mirror behind it. The villain would then mesmerize the hero with whispers of great riches if only . . . if only. But it would all end there, with the hero having seriously considered the proposal, then, of course, discarding it. Though the hero is down on his luck, as low as he's ever been, he knows to join in would only take him lower. What a story.

But it didn't happen that way. To eventually become something that we would live with full-time for almost two years, the beginning of the Libya deal was hardly something to sit up and take notice of. The old man was approached in July 1978 by a state senator from Georgia and a couple of other people. They met with him at the station and asked him if he would go to Libya as part of a "goodwill" trip, organized by the Libyan government, to help promote trade between the two countries. After first declining, my dad agreed. He was tired, he said, and thought a change would be good for him. And that's how it began.

I have to say I never liked the man who brought Libya into

our lives. He was a stereotypical Southern politician: mush-mouthed and loud and backslapping. And there was money on his mind when he came to Plains and fawned over my father. And, true to all men like him, as soon as any hint of contro-versy from the whole deal, *his* deal, hit the press, he backpedaled hard and scuttled away, leaving the old man vul-nerable from all sides. Other than that, the man is not much worth mentioning.

The first trip was scheduled for September 1978 and my father invited one of his best friends, Don Carter, to join him. Mr. Don is a well-known businessman in Georgia and researched Libya a bit before making his decision. After find-ing out about the strained, almost nonexistent relationship between the United States and Libya, not to mention Libya was considered to be the second-most dangerous place in the world for U.S. citizens, he decided not to go. He drove to Plains to try and talk my father into staying away, too. Of course, the old man didn't listen, even though my mother sat crying, begging him to at least think about it.

For five days, my father and Randy Coleman, another friend of our family, toured Libya, visiting farms and such and going to receptions. My father said nothing happened to indi-cate that the trip was anything more than what it appeared to be, a goodwill trip. He left thinking there just might be some-thing to involving himself with the import/export business and began making plans to receive a delegation from Libya in Georgia. Innocent as hell, he thought.

The press saw it another way and jumped on him feet first when he returned home. The media, who had been amused and entertained by my father at first, suddenly turned vicious. Some columnists, proving themselves to be the ill-natured bastards I'd always suspected them of being, began viewing each and every inept attempt my father made to enter the world of global finance as part of a vast conspiracy involving my uncle. The old man deserved some of it, surely, but definitely not all. And he didn't stand a chance when the press decided to unload on him. Who would? They badgered him constantly; stalking him and shoving microphones and cameras in his face. And then he made the infamous "There are more Arabs than Jews" statement, and all hell broke loose. My father's days of good ol' boy celebrityhood were over.

He was an official pariah, and if the sounds of people backing away and disassociating themselves could be heard, we would have all been deafened. Appearances were cancelled; phone calls from him were ignored. That one state senator was caught on camera, bumbling and fumbling and sounding all the world like Foghorn Leghorn: "I told ol' Billy, I say, I told him, boy, you ain't a' gonna catch me dealin' with no *A*-rabs. No suh! I say, no suh!" And then he vanished. As queasy as we were from what my father was up to, the sight of all those fair-weather friends treating him like shit, if possible, made us even sicker.

One of the episodes with the press, comical in a way, epitomizes how eager some of them are for a story, any story. My father and a few others were waiting at the airport for the Libyan delegation. A reporter had been invited to witness the arrival. Of course, as they sat in their cars beside the runway, my old man was drinking. When he stepped out to take a leak, after hours of waiting, the reporter thought it was a good idea and decided to relieve himself, too. To any man born and raised in the country, taking a piss outside is as natural as breathing. And if there are no ladies present, or the eyes of the more uptight in our society aren't upon you, it is rarely given a second thought. So the old man zipped up, never realizing the next day he would read about how uncouth and crude he was, about how appalled the reporter was at seeing the brother of the president of the United States take a piss beside the runway in Atlanta. Never mind it was at night. Never mind my father thought he was among friends. The asshole reporter just had to let the world know what kind of a monster my old man *really* was.

I stayed away when the Libyans came to Georgia. I was already sick of hearing about them and wished they would just go away. No one in the family could figure out what was going on, and the old man sure as hell didn't feel the need to explain. And by the time January 1979 rolled around, he was so deep into the pit of his alcoholism that you couldn't talk to him anyway. Truthfully, I was sicker of him than anything else going on.

I remember going to the house in Buena Vista, the house that had become more a prison for my mother than a home, to get some clothes washed. The place felt lifeless. My mother was at the kitchen table, with a cup of coffee between her hands, staring out the window. She didn't smile much anymore; didn't throw her head back and laugh and laugh when I teased her. She didn't know it then, but my father had dragged her down into that pit with him. All of us were down there, unable to escape the embrace of the old man's alcoholic bearhug. It seemed everyone had pleaded with him to get help: my mother, my grandmother, and his good, close friends. But nothing penetrated his brain: not crying, not begging, not the fact he had a two-year-old son running around he barely recognized. Nothing.

My father was sitting in his chair in the little room off his bedroom. Just sitting. Like a great, bloated toad he sat. His skin was gray and there was a sheen of sweat on his forehead. He was fat and swollen and he reeked of alcohol. No solid food had passed his lips in over a month. All of his nourishment came from a bottle. I spoke, but he didn't; unaware, as far as I know, that I was even in the room. He just sat there with no life in his eyes, only insanity.

And, God help me, at that moment I wished he would die. Die, I wished, and take all of the shit you've piled on us with you. Do one good thing, die.

I've wished a million times since I could take that moment away.

Our family doctor and good friend, Dr. Paul Broun, had been trying to convince my father to go into treatment for years and, like everyone else, didn't have any luck. Fortunately, yes, fortunately, my father developed a severe case of bronchitis and his stomach began to bleed. Both were illnesses he could admit to and agreed to let Dr. Paul treat him for them. But first, Dr. Paul told him, you'll have to go through detox. The old man, being who he was, figured a few days without alcohol would be easy. It was hell.

For eleven days my father laid strapped to the bed with tubes running from his body, sweating and having seizures and vomiting. He screamed and ranted and watched bugs and spiders crawl the wall. The devil sat beside him and laughed. He cursed my mother, who stayed with him through it all, and anyone else who entered the room. He clawed and scratched. He threw things. And then he slept. When he woke, he wanted a drink.

While my father was walking through his nightmare, plans were being made to get him into rehabilitation. Captain Joseph Pursch, chief of the Alcohol Rehabilitation Service at Long Beach Naval Hospital in Long Beach, California, knew what my father needed and called the White House. My uncle, commander in chief, reactivated my father in the Marine Corps so he would be eligible for admission to a military hospital. If I had ever doubted my uncle's love for my father, I never would again.

The old man wasn't aware of the plans to get him into treatment, but when he found out, he tentatively agreed. When it began to look like a sure thing, however, my father panicked a bit. He came up with his own agenda and devised a plan to flee to Venezuela. The fact that he was actually willing to give up everything he ever knew just so he could drink in peace still amazes me. The disease is *that* insidious. His mistake came with casually mentioning to my mother he just felt *uncomfortable* traveling without his passport, even on a trip inside the country. He never had even a slim chance of becoming an expatriate, though. There were so many people surrounding him when he boarded the plane to California, he was barely able to breathe. Friends and family members had tried too hard getting him to that point, and there was no way they were going to allow him to bolt.

So, beginning in February 1979, he stayed at the Long Beach treatment center for nine weeks. So did my mother, who was surprised to learn she, too, was expected to go through treatment. "But I don't drink," she said, "and have no reason to be here. Billy's the one with the problem, not me." It was then we first learned alcoholism extends well beyond the person sucking down the booze. It is a family problem, a problem that won't just up and go away because the main offender quits drinking. My mother found out that she, for all the years of thinking of herself as the good Southern wife, had been "enabling" my father, as had we all, with the excuses and the white lies and the pretending-not-to-notice turns of our heads. So she stayed, and learned it was okay not to put up with the old man's shit anymore.

My father wanted me to come out for a week. Please, my mother said, he asked me to ask if you would come. I did, but I hated every minute of it. The old man had been gone a month and he was slim and he was tan and was trying hard to grow a moustache. Our reunion was tentative and my father seemed shy at first. Maybe it was shame. At the time, I hoped so. I was still a long way from any forgiving stage and doubtful I would ever even come close. Oh, I was glad for my father, happy he'd chosen the treatment, but suspicious of his sincerity. I thought I knew him too well and figured he only quit drinking out of spite. I imagined him saying to himself, "All right, Goddammit. All of you think I can't stop if I want to? Okay. I'll show you all." Years later, I found out that that was exactly what was going through his head. He said so himself and admitted to not taking his sobriety to heart the first several years after he quit drinking. So I was still leery of anything my father did. As far as I was concerned, I'd have to see to believe.

We'd been through too much shit of his making and I remembered it all. The most recent being his treatment as an alcoholic. He was a public figure and so were all of his problems. Hell, I could stand everybody knowing he was running around the country drunk as a coot. At my age, it gave me a certain badge that I wore proudly for a while. I liked hearing my peers point me out and say, "See him? His daddy's one partying son-of-a-bitch!" That, I could deal with. But the morning of the day he left for Long Beach, I was walking through the Student Center at Georgia Southwestern on my way to class. There were speakers in the ceiling and a local radio station was playing. News time came and one of the stories was about the old man going away to be treated for alcoholism. And like in a bad movie, everyone in the Student Center grew quiet as I walked by, looking at me. I could feel the eyes on my back as I passed, and I heard imagined whispers. The only thing to do is to look ahead and keep moving; hoping with every step that the worst was over.

But, of course, it wasn't. Turns out we were only at halftime.

The Libya Thing was far from over. In fact, it'd only just begun.

When the old man came back from treatment, a lot of us fully expected him to settle down, make a few apologies here and there, then go back to being a minor celebrity on the talk and game show circuit. He instead proceeded to set himself up as a commission agent for Libyan crude oil coming into the United States. That one deserved a double take. It turned out that the only thing different about my father after treatment was that he didn't drink anymore. He was still as hardheaded as ever and determined to do whatever the hell he wanted. The next year was filled with a series of trips to Europe for my father to negotiate the deal, and two more trips to Libya.

I went on one of those trips to Libya, along with my mother and several friends of the family. Everything went smoothly until we landed. It was night, and the airport was in the middle of the desert, miles away from Tripoli. The first indication we weren't in Kansas anymore was all the soldiers with Uzi machine guns standing around. The second was when all of us were separated and put into individual cars, then whisked away into the night. We all met up about an hour later, after tearing through the desert, at a small brick building somewhere, and were escorted to a room piled with pillows and carpets on the floor. Each of us was questioned as to who we were, even though the guy knew exactly who he was talking to. We found this out when he would correct our answers by glancing at the clipboard he carried. Finally, hours after landing, we were taken to our hotel and woke the next morning to the sounds of the call to prayer echoing throughout the city. I looked out the window and knew immediately I was a long, long way from home. We were in a hotel on the Mediterranean and it was beautiful. There was just so much to see from that window and my fear from the night before had eased away. My parents had a suite a few doors down with a balcony. Clarence Gibbons, a friend of ours who worked for CBS, was standing with his camera, taking pictures of MIGs flying formation out over the ocean. The door to the room burst open and two soldiers with guns came in, demanded the camera, and took Clarence's film away. They couldn't speak English, but they communicated pretty well. Our interpreter, Mohammed Burki, told us there was a Libyan naval base down the way and that the government was a little sensitive about Americans taking pictures of their fighter jets. Nobody had to be told twice.

From that moment on, the fact I was in an exotic land, a land I'd only experienced through TV or movies, was overshadowed by a constant paranoia. I saw wonderful and strange things, ate weird foods, and walked through bazaars that were much older than the country I'd come from. But I couldn't enjoy any of it. I was scared to death. The reason we were in Libya was to attend the Tenth Anniversary of the Tenth of September Revolution, when Qaddafi came to power. Part of the celebration involved an eight-hour military parade. Let me write that again. An *eight-hour* military parade. Complete with tanks and missiles and thousands of soldiers from countries sympathetic to Qaddafi. We were told more than a million people were present, and the roar when the colonel himself stepped up to the podium was deafening. He was in uniform, medals and all, and surrounded by his personal guard, about five hundred red-bereted, armed soldiers. He allowed the celebrants to cheer him for a while, then raised his hand. Silence. Instantly. He spoke for an hour, taking the crowd to the edge of frenzy before lifting his hand for quiet. Those of us on the bleachers behind him all wore headphones and everything was interpreted for us. But I don't remember any of the speech. The situation was too surreal for me to do anything but sit and think of where I was.

And the whole trip, my father kept pointing out things to me and my mother, telling us how great everything was. It was as if he was trying hard to convince himself of something and wanted us to reaffirm his decision to come. I wasn't buying any of it. I wanted to go home.

I don't remember much about our tours of the schools and the farms and the quarries and such. I didn't pay attention, really. All I could think about was the day we were going to leave. One thing I do remember is an episode in my parent's suite at the hotel. All of us had gathered there to put our feet up and rest a bit. Someone had packed a big suitcase full of American snack foods and we were digging through it, tired of goat testicles, camel heart, and couscous. Mohammed Burki, our interpreter, was with us and he inquired about the cans of Vienna sausages. He ate five or six, declaring them delicious. Clarence Gibbons eased over to the table, picked up the empty can and peeled the label off. He then quietly walked over to a trashcan and tore the label into tiny pieces. "What are you doing?" I asked. He shook his head, glancing over at Burki. "Pork," he whispered.

I was glad when we left. And I never want to go back again.

The old man worked out a deal with Charter Oil Company to work with him with the Libyans. He also asked for a loan of $500,000 to tide him over until the deal was complete. All together, he received $220,000 as a loan from the Libyans, who are not necessarily considered to be on par with your friendly neighborhood bank. In April 1980 the deal was completed, and the Libyan government sent a confirmation cable to Charter Oil. Our government got hold of the cable, got pissed off, and asked my father to stop doing whatever he was doing. The deal fell apart. The old man was asked to register as a foreign agent to Libya and refused. Of course the press picked up on the foreign agent thing, failing to mention that tens of thousands of people in our country are "foreign agents." The term has no more ominous meaning than that a person has business dealings with another country. But it was just too good of a thing for the media to pass up. The *president's* brother? A *foreign* agent? Oh my! *How* could such a thing *be*? And then some of the asshole columnists began insisting there had to be links to Jimmy. There were none, but still the Senate held hearings on the matter.

The press, original as ever, labeled the whole thing "Billygate." I spent a few years believing the investigation was politically motivated by the Republicans. And I was sort of right. While many Republicans gleefully watched what was going on with my father and never missed a chance to comment on it, it's a known fact that there were several powerful Democrats who also wanted my uncle out of the White House. My father, I believed, was used as a tool to try and embarrass his brother. The funny part was that my old man was doing one hell of a job on his own.

The hearings were a joke. A thirty-million-dollar joke. They were televised and Arthur Cheokas, another fine friend of the family, and I sat in his liquor store and watched part of the proceedings. The door opened to the room where the hearings were held and a man entered carrying a piece of paper in his hand. He walked to the table and whispered into the ear of one of the senators. The camera panned back and forth from my father to the row of oh-so-pure-as-snow gentlemen questioning him. The senator straightened in his seat and spoke gravely into the microphone. Something to this effect: "We have another development here. Mr. Carter, were you aware so-and-so, a good friend of yours, is a known *cocaine* dealer?" Then he glared. I swear, my father's face drained of blood. He was pale white and began to stutter. The hearing went into recess for the day. The next morning's papers carried headlines declaring my father to be connected with international drug dealers. As it turned out, a friend of the son of one of my father's acquaintances had once been arrested for possession. Naturally, the papers explained this on page fifty-seven of the business section the following day, if they explained it at all.

During the course of the investigation, the old man was pegged as being involved in everything from drug dealing to arms trading. None of it was true. The only thing my father was guilty of was making a bad, bad mistake in choosing whom to go into business with. I have transcripts of the hearing, but more interesting are the copies of correspondences between those on the committee. There is a general tone of "What the hell's going on here? Why are we wasting our time on this?" about them. In the end, after spending so much money and time on the matter, they had to do something. Which pretty much amounted to them all shaking their fingers at my father and saying, "Bad Billy! . . . Bad!"

I guess they went back to their jobs of running the country all aglow from a job well done. But it wasn't over for my old man. He was flat broke and had no job.

And he still had the IRS to contend with.

My father was no stranger to the IRS. They actually began their investigation of the family when Jimmy first ran for president. Someone was determined to prove that there was no way he could've been elected without money being funneled from the family business to his campaign. This was the first of many allegations that proved to be false. But throughout the four years Jimmy was in office, they kept pecking. When it came out that the old man had taken money from the Libyans, the IRS pounced on him. They demanded all the records from the warehouse, which had been in the hands of the grand jury investigators for a couple of years, the ones checking into the alleged misuse of campaign funds. When this was explained, the IRS said, "Too bad. That another government agency is in possession of files we want is no excuse for you not giving them to us. Hmm. You'll be fined, let's see, a thousand dollars a day until you cough them up." Then they demanded the taxes be paid on the money he received from the Libyans, money that was considered a loan by my father. Of course he didn't have it. At the time, he was trying to pay four different law firms representing him in a number of different things. Things, for the most part, brought down on his head by your friend and mine, the United States government. The Libyan deal was being looked into by three different law enforcement agencies from three different angles. And there was the accusation of international arms trading and the charge of cavorting with known terrorists, both of which just *had* to be investigated. Of course, there were those who were convinced he was getting special favors from Jimmy, and that rumor had to be thoroughly inspected, too. And no one fights the IRS alone. Each and every one of those charges, no matter how small, no matter how asinine, required its own team of attorneys. Big-time lawyers.

So my parents had reached a point where they were financially devastated. My mother, used to going to Piggly Wiggly every Saturday, filling her cart with enough food to feed a family of eight, then writing a check for it, had to wait for my father to come up with forty or fifty dollars cash each week to sustain the four of them still living at home. All their checking and savings accounts were frozen, their property was taken, and a chain was stretched across the driveway to their home in Buena Vista with a big red sign on it, warning everyone away under the penalty of getting their ass jumped on by the IRS, too. The doors and windows on the house were padlocked and sealed. Those IRS boys did one hell of a job in their search for nonexistent fraud. Such a good job that two of the agents investigating my father's case quit in protest at what they saw as needless harassment of him.

The IRS won, of course. All the property they seized was put up for auction. If not for friends of my father—Don Carter, Nookie Meadows, Arthur Cheokas, and Jimmy Murray—he would have lost everything. When they saw he was tired of fighting, and had decided to let it go, they got together and paid the IRS. Tom T. Hall gave concerts, and his wife, Miss Dixie, held a seemingly perpetual yard sale. Together they raised fifty thousand dollars and turned it in to the government on behalf of the old man. If not for all those people, and many, many others, I don't know what would have happened. All the property except for my parents' house was still sold off, it had to be, but instead of the IRS just taking what they could get for it, my father's friends got what it was worth. There was even a little left over. The station went, too. But it wasn't the same. The new owner didn't renew the beer license. And the station without beer is, well, like the station without beer.

My version of the Libya Thing and the IRS mess is pretty condensed. I've left out many details involving both incidents, a lot of which I can't remember at all. Some from one even bleed over into the other because the timelines overlap. Not to mention the campaign funding investigations. Those two or three years became a blur. It seemed that every day the old man was being slapped with a subpoena. Our phones were tapped, badly. The FBI or the IRS or the grand jury investigators, pick one, put a tiny little trailer on the corner of my parents' property and tapped directly into the phone line. You could hear them when you picked up the receiver. We learned to curse them like dogs before dialing. And when my father left home each day, he had his own motorcade. Five unmarked cars waited for him around the clock on the county road at the edge of his property, making no attempt at being discreet. My father called me from a pay phone once when I was living in Americus. "Meet me at the crossroads in Webster County at seven o'clock tomorrow morning," he said. "Leave your engine running and have the door open." I'd become used to cryptic calls by this time. At seven that next morning, as I stood beside my truck, I looked down the road and saw movement. A minute later, the old man's black El Dorado appeared out of a cloud of red dust. He jumped out, dove into my truck, yelled at me to haul ass and then took off. I'd already been coached and headed back towards Americus, taking my time and stylin' in the Cadillac. Sure enough, after my old man was a minute and a half ahead in his getaway and safe, his five-car entourage appeared in my rearview mirror. They followed me, catching on only when I pulled into the parking lot at school. A point for the good guys.

A lot of people have asked me why my uncle didn't step in and put a stop to all the investigations and the harassment of my father. I wondered, too. After it was all over, years later, I found the courage to ask. The old man became angry with me. "That's a stupid question," he said. But, why, I wanted to know, why didn't he pick up a phone and stop it? "Because he couldn't," my father said. "He just couldn't." He didn't say any more. I had to figure it out for myself. Jimmy just couldn't. It was a no-win situation. Any move my uncle made to help my father out of his troubles would've definitely been looked at as an abuse of his office. The press would have gladly seen to that. Both Jimmy and my father knew this and understood it. It was a painful time for them.

It was years before I realized I'd overlooked the most amazing part of this story. When the real shit storm hit, my father was only a few months out of treatment. I've honestly marveled time and again at how he kept from crawling back into the pit. A lot of other people would've stuck their heads up, tested the wind, then made a trip to the nearest liquor store, never again to face the world sober. But, then, a lot of other people weren't the old man.

One thing that kept him going through this time was all the people around the country who saw a bit of themselves every time they looked at the old man. Regardless of his problems, they still thought of him as one of them. He was still a blue-collar hero of sorts—a cult figure. This was proven over and over by the letters he received and by the number of people who stopped him on the streets to shake his hand and to tell him to hang on, give 'em hell. They still believed in him. And when the 1980 election rolled around he was, once again, a big draw at campaign events. But, in their wisdom, the people running the campaign, the professional hacks, thought it would be better if the old man kind of stayed away. They decided not to use one of the best campaign tools they had. Let's pretend, they told each other, that the president doesn't even have a brother. Though Jimmy didn't know about it, they asked my father if he would mind not attending the 1980 Democratic Convention. As a matter of fact, *told* him not to come.

There are those, blood kin even, who claim that if not for my father, Jimmy would have been reelected president in 1980.

Well . . . fuck 'em.

Chapter Seventeen

In most stories, this chapter would be the one about how everybody finally breathed a sigh of relief and then settled down to live happily ever after. Jimmy was out of office and the spotlight was dimming rapidly. This was a good thing or a bad thing, depending on how you looked at it. My father was scheduled for appearances before several groups investigating several different things. But within a week after the November elections, he received telegrams from all those investigating him. Everything was dropped. Just like that, the investigations were over. Nah . . . It wasn't political.

Every day, fewer and fewer tourists made their way to Plains. Before long, one or two of the town dogs could be seen checking out a spot in the middle of Main Street for an afternoon nap. Those town folks who had bitched and moaned in the beginning about the changes taking place in Plains were now bitching and moaning about the economic decline. Somehow, the family got blamed for that, too. But things were slowly getting back to some semblance of what they once were. Except for my family, that is.

I've had people comment to me on how hard it seems to get
to know my family now. We're standoffish, I've been told, distant to those we're not familiar with. And it's true, to a point.
Though my mother is hospitable to a fault and all of my sisters could be poster girls for Southern manners, there came a
time when all of us developed a siege mentality of sorts. We
had to. Time after time after time, it seemed my family was
tested; our world was threatened. The need to protect became
strong. Trust was something you no longer gave freely. And all
because of those four years. Four years that became a blur; a
great mess of towering highs and horrible lows, from the
excitement of being thrust into the center of national attention, to the pain in the pit of the stomach from watching our
father devastated and humiliated, from witnessing his transformation into a great, sad joke. *We* knew who he was and
how it hurt him. It had to be a tripling of the pain the rest of
us felt. At least we could get out of the way and maybe hide
for a while. But *he* couldn't.

I think some of the worst moments in those years were
when someone, anyone, would look upon my father with pity.
Pity was the last thing he wanted. And he was embarrassed,
horribly so. It's hard for anyone to believe this about my old
man. He appeared in public to be the same old guy with the
cut-you-to-ribbons wit who was discovered by the press five
years before. But not with us. With us, he withdrew, continued to shut down when the family was around. It was as if he
was suspicious of what we might be thinking of him; that
maybe, in our eyes, we all thought he'd somehow fallen. And,
yes, there were times when I thought that way about him,
times when I denied kinship, but those times never lasted for
long. Hell, he was the old man.

I wanted to grab him by the shoulders and shake him and
tell him to wake up. "You went through some horrible shit," I

wanted to say, "and came out the other side. You're still standing." I wanted to tell him he taught me things; that I admired
him for hanging on. But I didn't. I am my father's son.

No, it wasn't a brand-new beginning for the old man, not
then. He'd lost a lot more than just money or property. His self
worth was what he was looking for, and he couldn't really
begin anything without it.

He needed a job. There were lawyers to pay. In June 1981,
a man named Don Tidwell, a mobile home manufacturer from
Alabama, decided to ignore all the negative press about my
father and take a chance on him. I think he, along with a lot
of other people, were amazed to find out the old man was not
the idiot the press made him out to be. Before long he was a
regular at the industry shows; he was once again a draw. At
first I'm sure it was for novelty's sake that the mobile home
dealers sought him out, a kind of morbid curiosity. But the old
man immersed himself in the business and became more than
just a sideshow attraction. He became an expert and more
than earned his keep.

The change in him was amazing. It seemed he'd found a
place to settle. In the mobile home manufacturing business he
was a lot more than the brother of a former president of the
United States; he was a respected man in the business whose
opinion was valued. And he still rated a paragraph or two and
a photo in the local papers when he visited towns promoting
Tidwell homes. People came to the mobile home lots to see
him and to get his autograph and to tell him about the time
they saw him on the Merv Griffin show and about how the
IRS are a bunch of sonsabitches. They brought empty Billy
Beer cans to show him and laughed nervously when they told
him how bad they thought it was. Uncountable families gathered to have their pictures taken, and the old man would stand
for hours, surrounded by mobile homes and free hot dogs and

soft drinks and balloons for the kids, grinning like hell. And the people left happy, sometimes after only incidentally checking out the trailers and talking to the lot owner about filling out a credit application. The old man hadn't lost it. People, *real* people, still wanted him around.

We thought he was back. And on the surface, he was. He'd found something to do with his life and gave it everything he had. The job required him to travel five or six days a week doing promotions, and he loved it. The only drawback was that, for the most part, Mama and my younger sister and brother were left alone at the house in Buena Vista. The company would fly them to Haleyville, Alabama, though, to be with him every once in a while.

I left Georgia in early 1981, moved to Tennessee, and tried to hide for a while. All of us were shell-shocked a bit at what we'd been through. Though my mother, my sisters, and I had only been on the fringes of things during those four years, we were all exhausted. We'd had enough. It was one hell of an experience but, honest to God, not one I would wish on my worst enemy.

To hear the old man was doing well made me happy. He deserved it. It was time to exhale and move on down the road.

I met a girl named Marlene Sweazey shortly after I moved to Tennessee and we got married in July 1982. We had all kinds of plans. And then my father called, used his powers of persuasion, and convinced me I was missing out on the chance of a lifetime if I didn't follow him and become one of the legions of people entering the wonderful world of mobile homes. Trailer trash, as those of us in the business called ourselves. To this day, I can't honestly say why I agreed to join him, or even why he asked. Maybe there was something left over from the days at the warehouse when both of us thought our futures were set solid in the red dirt of Plains. Maybe he felt as though he still owed me a future or maybe I felt as though I owed him one. I suspect, though, it was by force of will on his part. I was grown and three hundred miles away, but I could still feel the pull of his personality. Whatever the case, I went.

For a while I worked on a retail mobile home lot in Ft. Walton Beach, Florida. Then, in 1982, the old man left Tidwell Homes and went to work for Scott Housing Systems in Waycross, Georgia, as vice president of marketing. Again, I followed. My folks bought a house there and began living like a family again. Marlene and I got an apartment not far from them. Working in the mobile home business was not something I had ever imagined myself doing, but it was a start and things began to settle down a bit.

Very quickly, it became apparent the old man was a workaholic, close to obsessed with his job. Everything he did, everybody he talked to or hung out with, was related to the business. Workdays for him began as they had when he ran the warehouse, at 4 A.M., and ended only when no one else was at the office. He did his job very, very well and became a star of sorts in the industry. He was balls-to-the-wall, eaten up all to hell with selling and promoting mobile homes. This was good for the company and good for him, but pure hell on my mother. She was not happy in Waycross.

It didn't seem possible, but my father's moods became blacker and deeper when he was at home, saving the good parts of himself only for those not related. My wife, Marlene, was almost amused by our attitude towards my father, basically wondering why all of us just didn't tell him to kiss our asses. The old man seemed to sense this, and she became one of the few in the family who could deal with him without fearing his temper.

My mother and Mandy and Earl began tiptoeing around

him at home again, careful not to upset him. He'd come home from work, eat supper, then sit in his chair, reading and brooding, until he went to bed. The next day at work, he'd once again be joking and laughing and taking care of business. Then he'd walk through the door at home and shut down again, a heavy, uncomfortable silence rolling off of him. It was almost as if the last thing he wanted to see was those in the family being happy in his presence.

One Thanksgiving, all of my sisters and brothers-in-law and nieces and nephews came to Waycross. My mother was ecstatic, having been too far away from the grandbabies for too long. We all gathered at my folks' house and there my father sat, in his chair, brooding. He didn't really acknowledge anyone. But we didn't care, it was a holiday and my mother was happy. I'll never know why, but the old man got up and put a cassette of a harelipped motivational speaker in the stereo and cranked the volume to full level. I, along with everybody else, was stunned. My father sat on the floor in front of the stereo, ignoring my mother's pleas to turn it off and seemingly engrossed in listening to "Make a million nollars my meing all you can me" blaring from the speakers. Very bizarre, to say the least.

The most troubling part about how my father was acting was that there was nothing for us to pin it on. Alcohol was out of the picture and had been since he left Long Beach. Federal agents weren't lurking in bushes outside of his home anymore, and he seemed to really enjoy his work. The only thing any of us could figure out, and this was later, was that he'd been more deeply affected by his years of ups and downs than any of us could come close to imagining. And, in spite of all the times we tried to tell him different, he couldn't see that the things he'd done in the past didn't matter anymore. Or he *wouldn't* allow himself to see it.

Not every single day was bad. The old man seemed to find great joy in my little brother, Earl, and spent a good deal of time with him. And, true to form, as in everywhere he went, my father formed several great friendships in Waycross. He also found a lot of time and opportunity to follow one of his passions, which was poker. I never knew him to pass up a hand. There's a lot of money to be made in the mobile home business, and there were times when I stood amazed on the sidelines, watching my father and four or five other big dogs feign disinterest in a kitty that equaled half my yearly wage. Through the years he'd won land, a Tennessee Walking horse, and several automobiles, not to mention wads of cash.

The mobile home industry runs on flash and big financial deals. It can be brutal, especially to those who are salesmen on the manufacturing end. It's high pressure for everyone involved. If you don't sell homes, you don't eat, and rarely is anyone carried after a couple of months of poor showings. My father became the unofficial hatchet man in the company, and a call to his office for an unscheduled meeting was a reason to fear losing your job. He could be cold about it and claimed to like chewing someone's ass for not carrying their weight. Every day, more and more of the old Billy Carter was lost to whatever it was he was trying to find. A little bit of the man he was at home began to creep out at work. The hard man, the brooding man, was going public.

I was not a salesman. I worked directly with the purchasing agent, figuring out materials and costs needed to build the houses. But the tension was still there. We were competing with many other manufacturers for the mobile home market and constantly looking for some way to trim a few dollars here and there. I found myself almost as caught up with the business as my father was, but for a different reason. I didn't want to disappoint the old man and worried constantly that something I did was going to cost the company a lot of money. There came a time when if any hint of an error on my part came to light, I found myself unreasonably terrified. The thought of walking down the hall to face the old man from across his desk made me sweat. And I wasn't the only one. Men older than I had gone into his office and left, minutes later, with tears in their eyes. I hated it. A few months after the birth of our first son, Will, I asked to be transferred to the Tennessee plant to work on the line. The old man didn't like it a bit, but I had to go. I needed some peace.

The two things that altered my father's life during the time he lived in Waycross much more than his becoming a workaholic were the deaths of his sister Ruth and his mama, Miss Lillian. Aunt Ruth died of pancreatic cancer in September 1983. Grandma followed just over a month later, dying of complications from breast cancer. Though Aunt Ruth was older by seven years, she and my father were the two babies of their family. She was the one who called during the times of all of his troubles just to talk. Not about Libya or the IRS or about alcoholism, but about the things brothers and sisters speak of. She was one of his greatest defenders, and losing her was a blow I didn't think he could recover from.

And then Grandma, that great lady, passed away only a few weeks later. She was eighty-five and in her life had done more than most could hope for in twice the years. The people she'd touched and helped to heal and wrapped in her compassion, many a world away in India, were uncountable. One of those people was my father. Her presence alone calmed him, gave him peace. Even when things were at their worst for him, when he was fighting off all the things trying to beat him down, he always found the time to go and sit with Grandma. Just to sit. With Grandma he was never questioned, never badgered, and never judged. She loved him unconditionally and her death damn near took him to his knees. I don't think any us of really knew the strength of the bond between my father and my grandmother. Just a hint came a few years after her death when doctors found a cancerous mass in my sister Jana's leg. My oldest sister, Kim, was at the hospital with my father when they found out. "Daddy picked up the phone," she said "and began to dial a number. He put it down a few seconds later, telling me he'd forgotten. 'I used to call her first about everything', he told me. He'd tried to call Grandma two years after she'd died."

My father insisted my grandmother's body be taken back to the Pond House, a place she loved, the day before the funeral. Some rolled their eyes at this, telling him, "That's just not done anymore, Billy." But they brought her back and my father stayed alone with her all that night, sitting, just sitting, for one last time.

Towards the end of 1985, the old man decided to go into business for himself. With a partner, he launched a chain of retail mobile home lots. He called me and wanted me to go to work for him. Of course, even though there was a little voice inside my head calling me a dumb-ass, I moved my family from Tennessee back down to Georgia. The job lasted for all of six months, time enough for me to witness the seedy side of the business. My dad and his partner didn't get along and the partner bought him out. Then he declared bankruptcy and left my father stuck with one hundred thousand dollars in debt run up when they were still doing business together. I began to think that if I squinted real hard, and held my head a certain way, I could discern a long line of people forming, waiting their turn to take a swing at the old man.

Ocilla Industries, out of Fitzgerald, Georgia, hired him to run Arabi Homes, their modular home division. Again, I went with him, having no job, no money, and no way to get back to

Tennessee, where I truly wanted to be. My folks had moved back to Plains, buying a home adjoining Jimmy's property. Marlene and Will and I, after living in a trailer on Cow Pen Road for a while, rented a home a mile down 280 from them.

The night before my first day on the job, the old man said he'd be by the next morning to pick me up. He pulled into our driveway at 4 A.M. Arabi was sixty miles away and the silence of the ride was broken only by an occasional heavy sigh from my father. We didn't leave the plant that evening until seven o'clock. Again I witnessed how his demeanor changed around those not in the family. With them, he was funny and entertaining and could keep a roomful enthralled for hours with his stories. When we left for the ride home, though, that scowl of a mask would descend and the sighs would come. I dreaded those two-hour round trips. They ended for me when he started wanting to leave for work at 3, sometimes 2:30 A.M. I drove myself from them on. My father continued to work sixteen- and eighteen-hour days, coming home only to eat and to brood. It was as if being at home with his family was painful to him and the black moods he lived in seeped from his body, clinging to anyone who walked through the door. Though my father had not touched a drop of alcohol since his treatment, there were times when I almost wished I could find him passed out in the yard, cradling an empty vodka bottle in his arms. At least then we could all be relieved in knowing that the villain had been identified. To walk into my parents' house when my father was there became a challenge; the energy expended watching every move we made around him was exhausting. My father was dry, but he wasn't truly sober. Something had to give.

I had a small office at Arabi Homes where I worked on cost estimates for new projects. One day my father came in and shut the door. It scared me. "Jana has cancer," he said. And he cried and cried. I had rarely seen a tear fall from my father's eye and I wanted to hug him. But I didn't and couldn't remember if I ever had. Jana had the malignant tumor removed from her leg and is doing fine now. I don't think she knows it, but her illness helped create the first cracks in the shell my father had built around himself.

Dealing with my father, and seeing how his personality was grinding down those who loved him most, became too much for me to handle. I had to go. The trip up to his office was three days in the making. It took that long for me to grow the balls to face him. I told him I had a job offer in Tennessee. It was a lie; there was no job. He didn't speak and didn't have to. The look of betrayal on his face said all that needed saying. I felt as though I'd joined those waiting in that long, imaginary line.

My last day on the job he came down to my office and went through a box of personal effects I had gathered up. He said he wanted to make sure I wasn't stealing any company property. It hurt, but didn't really matter. Finally, I was free.

In leaving Plains, this time for good, I thought, I was leaving a lot of other shit behind. I worried for my mother and wanted her to get away, too. Leave, I told her, get away from him before he pulls you down again. But she smiled the way that only Mama could and shook her head. She loved him too much. She understood exactly, though, why I had to go and insisted that I do whatever it took to make my family and myself happy.

The relationship between my father and me was decidedly cold, and he wouldn't even come to the phone for a while when I'd call. But then strange things began to happen. Good things. Mama would tell me about the old man going to AA meetings regularly, something he'd let slide shortly after he left treatment. There was a difference in her voice; she sounded ... happy. And then one night the old man picked up the phone and we talked for hours. I can't remember a damned thing either of us said, we just talked. The novelty of it left us both a little stunned. My parents started giving interviews and speeches. Him about his life as an alcoholic and her about putting up with his shit for all those years. They were a hit. My father began to realize he had value as one who could help others who were struggling to understand and face their disease. I don't how or why, but in a period of a few short months, the old man looked in at himself, didn't like what he saw, and started climbing out. I cried one night when I hung up the phone. Not for any bad things I was feeling, but because I'd just talked to a man I'd been missing all of my life.

My folks came up to Tennessee for a visit that summer of 1987. They were passing through on their way to a seminar somewhere and couldn't miss a chance to see us and their friends, Tom T. and Miss Dixie. They were back and forth between the two houses for three days, and every meal we had together was an adventure. I remember watching my mother and father sitting on the sofa together. They sat close, touching each other, and laughing at the things each of them said. They talked about the appearances they had scheduled to talk to groups of alcoholics and about how the old man was getting offers again to do commercials and talk shows. He'd been approached about writing a book and was seriously considering it. They were happy and they were healthy and both were shining with a light only the truly content possess.

And then two months later Daddy was diagnosed with inoperable, pancreatic cancer.

Chapter Eighteen

I've heard, time and again, that God piles no more on you than he thinks you can handle. I hate that saying. Because in my father's case, it's hard for me to figure just who, exactly, was bearing the burden. At first telling, it seems as though my father was the one staggering beneath the weight. He was given a father he worshipped only to have him taken away when he was still a boy. His dream of carrying on where his father left off was granted briefly, only to have it, too, snatched away. He suffered the pain of public humiliation and the even greater pain of battling personal demons. God took his mama and his sister and threatened his daughter with cancer. And then when my father lifted his head to look out from beneath the load, when he straightened his back and shifted the weight and decided, yes, I can live with this, I have to, God laid his hand upon him and told him he would die.

But then I think about my mother and my sisters and my brother and me. We had the weight of watching his struggle; the weight of watching him make himself insane. We held our breath with every step he took, up or down, willing that if he slipped and fell his landing wouldn't be as brutal as the one before. And when he finally emerged from the pit he was in, not as a new man or a different man, but as the man all of us always knew was there, God laid another weight on us by taking him away.

* * *

"How's Daddy?" I asked my mother late that summer. I called at least once a week from Tennessee to keep up with what was going on in their lives. And I found I actually enjoyed talking to my father now; the tension was all gone. We *talked.*

"He's fine," she said. "I finally talked him into going to the doctor; he has an appointment tomorrow." The old man had been itching horribly and Mama said he had a yellowish cast to his skin. We were worried he might be suffering through some kind of heavy-duty allergies.

"Good," I told her. "Keep his old ass in line. Make him do what he's supposed to." She promised to let me know how everything turned out.

What she said a few days later was that Daddy had cancer. As torn up as she was about it, she told me not to worry because there was going to be an operation to remove the mass. We didn't know at the time that my father had been given a death sentence.

The surgery was to be done at Emory University Hospital in Atlanta. I drove down from Tennessee to be with him and the rest of the family, just the first of many weekend trips I was to make in the next year.

The hallway was full of kinfolk and friends waiting for word from the surgeon, and there was the definite feel of reunion floating about. We didn't see each other as much as we'd like anymore. And then the doctor came and told us that my father's cancer was inoperable.

My mother was by my father's side when he awoke, facing his look of expectation alone. She had to tell him the cancer had to stay where it was. But there were treatments they could try, she told him, and that's what they were going to do.

We all took our turns going in to visit him. I was scared and awkward when I entered the room, afraid of what I might see. But it was the old man, and he was as scared and as awkward as I was. We talked for a while and when time came for me to leave he told me he loved me. The first time ever.

The old man fought like hell. No one who knew him would have expected any less. The treatments he went through during the next year, some experimental, made him sick and weak but kept him going past the original three- or four-month prognosis. And he still, along with my mother, traveled around speaking about his alcoholism. That was something he wouldn't give up. I remember the calls from Mama, telling me about the hopes they had for new treatments and how she let herself sound excited for my sake.

It became almost a ritual for me to leave after work every Friday and travel down to Georgia. Not every weekend; my folks wouldn't let me. They didn't want me to take too much time from my family. But I went often, thinking my way down I-75, alone on the road at night.

I never asked my father what he was thinking about his cancer; the courage wouldn't come. It was only years later, when my wife was diagnosed with lung cancer in April 1998, that I began to think I even had an inkling of what was going through my father's head. You're alone in there, she told me, all by yourself with that thing in your body, thinking you used to live a life full of guarantees—guarantees of happy marriages and healthy babies and long productive lives. People with cancer, she said, know those guarantees are only illusion, and that the thing in their body is reality.

It's funny, the things a lonely nighttime ride can do inside your head. I'd begin the first of those trips always thinking of things that went on in my father's life. *All* the things, both good and bad. But then, for some reason, the bad things, the hurtful things, started to become small, small enough for me to hold in my hand and fling out the window if I chose. I've kept them, though, and have tucked them away. They are as much a part of my father as the good things.

I remembered the time the old man bought me a monkey, just because I *had* to have one. He sighed and puffed and raised hell, but he bought it. And then I remembered the times I'd seen him whisper in my mother's ear and make her throw her head back and laugh and laugh like no one else could. Or how he used to spend the weekend in Bermuda shorts and a Skylab Target T-shirt. I thought about how he stunned a perfect stranger, stranded beside the road a few miles from Plains, by lending the man his car. And how he loved board games and card games and would damn-near pout when he lost. I thought about his perfect grin. And I thought, wished maybe, that those silent rides with him when I was younger were silent because he was comfortable with my presence and didn't feel he had to speak. I thought of a lot of things, not the least of which was how lucky I'd been.

Each trip home told me a much different tale about my father than the ones who were with him every day were seeing. The slow movement I'd seen two weeks before became obvious weakness; the thinness became an alarming loss of weight. And then there came the time I walked through the door and he was sitting in his chair with an IV stand beside him. But still he talked; as much as he was able, he told his stories. And beside him, always, was Mama. She'd become expert at finding veins and dispensing the small miracles that keep the pain away. She lay beside him each night, rarely sleeping, as each movement my father made telegraphed its way to her. She knew, almost before he did, where the hurts were or what was needed to coax just a little more comfort into his body. And sometimes, she says, they both lay awake through the night, talking about things they'd never talked of before. For a year, my mother hurt when he hurt, laughed when he laughed, and cried when he cried.

There were ten million tiny ups and downs that year. Did Daddy eat today? No, not much. Your Daddy walked to the pond! He only stopped twice to rest! He hasn't slept well lately, he jerks a lot in his sleep and isn't getting any rest. Daddy went to see Earl play ball today and we stayed the whole game! Buddy, your daddy had to go back in the hospital this morning. I think you need to come home. Bring Marlene and Will this time. Come home and say goodbye.

Mama called me late the night of Thursday, September 22, 1988. I think it's time, she said. We left the next morning and arrived in Plains Friday evening. My father wanted to be at home and one of his friends had moved a hospital bed into my parents' bedroom. We walked back to see him and my son, William Alton Carter V, not yet three, climbed onto the bed with my father, William Alton Carter III, patted his face and told him that he loved him.

I don't remember much about the next twenty-four hours, except that the house was full of people coming to see my father. I got angry once at what I thought of as an intrusion into a family thing, but Mama pulled me aside and told me to remember that these people loved my father, too. And they did. Like me, most of them seemed to be expecting my father to somehow throw his blankets off, pull the tubes from his body and walk into the living room. God knows he seemed to be trying. Until he just couldn't anymore, he joked about what was going on around him. Every few minutes someone had to help him sit and hold a pan to his mouth. He said he was going to start charging admission, that no one was going to see him throw up for free.

Mama came out into the living room and told me that Daddy wanted to see me. I sat alone with him for a while and he told me things he wanted me to know; things he wanted me to do. Some things surprised me; some things made me love him even more.

That Saturday night, things grew quiet and my father slipped in and out of consciousness. We were all there in the bedroom with him. Daddy's sister, who we all called "Go-Go," and Miss Dixie were there, too. Mama sat beside the bed and held his hand. He woke once and asked us if we'd seen his daddy. "He was here," he said, "with Mama and Ruth. They're coming to get me in the morning." Then he slept again. He woke once more around midnight and looked in my mother's eyes. "I love you, Sybil," he said. Those were his last words.

None of us closed our eyes that night, worried he might slip away as we slept. We bumped around the house, one or two of us meeting in the kitchen from time to time for a cup of coffee and a hundred stories or more. But we always made it back to the bedroom.

And then his breathing slowed. The time between each rise of his chest seemed to stretch on and on and on. I found myself beside him, with my hand on his, trying to force my thoughts into his head. Breathe, goddammit! . . . Breathe! I thought, echoing his command to me on a nighttime ride more than twenty years before.

But it was morning.

His daddy had come to get him.

I went outside and sat beneath the gazebo, thinking about birds and breezes and waiting for the hurricane.

And I was laughing.

Summer 1998

It is August and we are going home for a few days.

Two or three times a year, my wife and I and our two sons travel the three hundred and twenty miles south from Tennessee, where we live, home to Plains. We all have different reasons for calling that small town home. I was born and raised there. And though I know I really don't, I think I own it. My wife, who was brought up in large cities and suburbs, found out there really were a few places seemingly untouched by the rest of the world in the short year she lived there and became enchanted. And though I think they don't yet know it, my sons are drawn there; tugged a bit by the red dirt running through their veins.

We leave the interstate just south of Birmingham and ease onto the familiar stretch of highway 280 East. And though still 170 miles away, I feel as if we are almost there. Because on this highway there are no more twists and turns. No more interstate exits. And this highway will lead us right to my Mama's front yard.

Overpasses and out-of-state tags give way to slow-moving

pick-up trucks and well-tended fields. And we become excited at glimpses of signs and scenes that mark the progress of our trip: four-acre flea markets, a billboard with a painted picture of Satan that reads "Go to CHURCH or the DEVIL will get YOU!," red earth, pecan trees, vast carpets of kudzu, and portable signs selling two-dollar watermelons and neck bones by the pound.

My sons become antsy and ask, over and over again, When are we going to get there? They believe there is something mystical about their Southern cousins, though they will lose their shine in a few days. And they both want to see what their "GrandmamainGeorgia" has stocked the cupboard with. They are only two of eleven grandchildren, each the favorite.

Before we were married, my wife had no sisters. Then mine adopted her. Now she has four. Five, really, because my mother adopted her, too. I think she is eager again to talk the talk of sisters. But more than that, I think she wants to make sure the town where dressed-up, little old ladies bring pies to your home and where the postmaster gives you chewing gum is still there.

I want to sit at the kitchen table, drink coffee with Mama, and talk about how things used to be. I want to see my sisters and my brother. I want to drive the dirt roads I know better than I know my name. And I want to talk to my dad.

Then we arrive and Mama is out the front door before we come to a stop. She has been waiting. And watching. And I'm sure she sensed us some thirty miles away, as only mamas can. Everybody hugs. Then my mother inspects my wife, asks her how she feels and tells her she looks "so gooood!" My sons, quiet for the first time in two hundred miles, have huge grins on their faces. They both act shy and duck their heads when Mama grabs them and says, "You better give me some sugar!"

They give her some sugar. We go inside and it is home. Mama says everybody will be over for supper. It seems our arrival is an event.

After we have rested a bit and settled in, I tell them I'll be back in a while. My sons want to come with me but my wife tells them to stay here, Daddy'll be back soon. She knows where I'm going.

I make a quick trip to the store and buy a single beer, hoping I won't see anyone I know just yet. There is ritual to visiting.

One mile west of town, on an old, familiar road, I park and sit for a moment. Waiting for something, I guess. When it doesn't come, I get out and walk the path to my father's grave. There are other stones here etched with my family name, but I pass those by. There will be other visitors.

Then I stand in front of, looking down at, my dad's marker. I pop the top and raise the beer and with a cheer I don't really feel, I say, "What's up, old man?"

And, as always, I calculate the months and years, represented by blank granite, between the dates of birth and death. He was young.

I sit on the ground, careful of the sand-spurs and red ants, and sip my beer. And I tell him about Marlene and about my sons. I talk about my writing and my job. I tell him Mama is okay, though she misses him. I tell him Earl is fine and bigger than me now but that I can still kick his ass. And then I tell him he was right about so many things and give belated thanks for past, unsolicited advice.

It is not right he should be so much easier to talk to dead than alive.

I notice fresh flowers by the headstone and remember how he started planting bulbs and trees and flowers after he got sick. Before, he'd never taken any interest in plants other than crops. It is sad to think it was in the few months before he died he discovered the *glory* of growth. Or maybe not. Maybe he found comfort in this discovery and surrendered easily, knowing his roots abound through us and ours and always would. I hope so.

Before I go, I reach in my pocket, pull out a new penny and place it, heads up, on the marker. Part of the ritual. There should be others; proof of past visits, but they are gone now. I can't help wondering if those vanished bits of copper fill the kitty in some celestial poker game played with my grandmother.

I raise my beer again and say, "Take care, old man."

Then I drive towards home.

It is suppertime.